Renewing your Mind

Renewing your Mind

Maintaining your Mental Health from a Biblical Perspective

Stephanie Jackson

Renewing your Mind

Dedications and Acknowledgements

This book is dedicated to My Lord and Savior Jesus Christ who healed me mind, body, and spirit; To the Holy Spirit who stuck by be through my struggles and strengthened me to write this book to encourage, exhort and uplift others, and to my 2 wonderful children who loved me unconditionally. You are my angels.

God has not given us a spirit of fear; but of power, and of love, and of a sound mind.
(2 Timothy 1:7, KJV)

Contents

Introduction

Your mind is your sacred place and learning how to control the thoughts that go into and out of your mind will help you maintain your mental health. Being mentally healthy will ensure that your mind and your life are places of peace and calmness. When your mind is filled with good thoughts it will be a place of peace and those closest to you will love to be around you and find you to be a blessing to have in their lives. On the other side of the coin, if your mind is a place filled with sadness, regret, shame, hatred, bitterness, anger, painful memories, and low self-worth, it will become diseased, and a diseased mind will lead to mental illness (or a mind illness). Living with these types of feelings and experiences in your mind will cause you to behave poorly, speak harshly to others, mistreat yourself, make bad decisions, and mistreat other people. When you interact with other people, and you have a diseased mind, those people will have an unpleasant experience. You must guard your mind and heart because all the issues of your life flows from these two places (1). God did not create your mind to be a place of torment, pain, or confusion. Learning to guard your mind and care for yourself mentally will ensure that you thrive and experience God's best in every other area of your life.

In his letter to the Romans the Apostle Paul admonishes the new believers there to "Be ye not conformed to this world: but be ye transformed by the renewing of your mind, that you may prove what is (that) good, and acceptable, and perfect will of God. (2). Paul clearly states here that the way to transform yourself (into a spiritually mature individual) is by renewing your mind. This book was written with the purpose of helping you learn how to guard your mind and, if necessary, renew your mind.

This book will help you understand the importance of mental health, how to maintain your mental health, and how to stop thinking self-defeating thoughts. This book is divided into 3 parts, and each part consists of 4 chapters. Part 1 is designed for younger readers who are learning how develop a healthy mind and develop healthy thought patterns. Part 1 will engage your mind, ignite your imagination, and allow you to view your mind as a sacred place that should always be guarded. Part 1 depicts the mind as a garden and the seeds as our thoughts, it will challenge you to use your imagination in a healthy way.

Part 2 of this book is designed for those who, like me, may have constantly indulged in negative thinking, possibly because they were raised in a family or community that was abusive and unsafe. Part 2 is also for individuals that did not learn how to guard their mind or practice good mental health habits for most of their lives and now find that their minds have become a place of torment. They now have a mind filled with overwhelming feelings of sadness, crippling anxiety, rage, depression, uncontrollable crying, constant feelings of dread and fear, profound hopelessness, and self-destructive thoughts. Having your mind filled with these thoughts will lead to behaviors that are harmful to yourself or your loved ones. Extreme behaviors and habits (that can develop because of a diseased mind) include drug or alcohol addiction, reckless spending, attaching yourself to toxic people and relationships, over-spending or over-eating and any other behaviors that cause emotional, mental, and physical distress. Part 2 of this book is designed to help lead you away from these negative raging thoughts in your mind back to the safe calm shores of mental wellness and peace.

Part 2 will teach you how to create stillness in your mind and in your environment. Just as Jesus spoke to the sea as the storm raged threating to sink the ship he was sailing in with his disciples and said "Peace! Be Still" (3) he will speak these same words to the raging thoughts and emotions in your mind. It is as simple as going to him in prayer and asking him to speak peace to your mind so that you can enjoy a life filled with his abundance, grace, and mental clarity. For 25 years I battled with negative raging thoughts in my mind. My mind (and life) was a place of extreme torment and mental anguish. I have also helplessly watched friends and loved ones as they were being overtaken by the same mental war, always wanting to help but never really knowing what to do or say to help them. Some of them have found mental peace, some are still fighting to find mental peace, and some of them are no longer alive. I do not say this to scare you but to drive home the importance of developing and maintaining a strong, sound, healthy mind.

Scriptures, personal experience, and professional knowledge will be utilized to back all the advice given in each of the sections in this book. I need you to understand how important it is to have an authentic personal relationship with God if you wish to be successful in maintaining your mental health. This relationship will help you maintain your mental health and it is also the best foundation to begin renewing your mind and rebuild your life. Part 2 of this book also shows you how to get rid of unhealthy ways of thinking and learn or re-learn how to think healthy thoughts. Through this book I am joining my faith with yours and extending my hand to you so that you know that you are not alone in this mental health journey. It is my sincere prayer that you learn how to develop a healthy mindset and begin to live the (more) abundant life that Jesus died for you to have (4).

The 3rd section of this book is for individuals, like me, who have surpassed the point of mental illness and have gone (or are going) into full mental breakdown, and this mental illness and breakdown has caused them to make poor decisions, decisions that are destroying their lives. Now, they must find the strength, courage, faith, and wisdom to renew their minds and rebuild their lives (as I have done and continue to do). The good news is, you can survive and recover from a complete mental breakdown. Not only can you survive a mental breakdown, but you can thrive afterward. Give your ashes and broken pieces to God and he will give you something beautiful in return (5).

Once you give those broken pieces to God and let him rebuild something beautiful, you will be able to accomplish great things. Yes, after a mental breakdown (and with the help of God) you can still write that book, start, or finish that degree, start your business, build wealth, and continue raising those children God blessed you with. I did all of this after my mental breakdown and as a single mother of two children. Yes, through Christ, there is a life filled with mental clarity, spiritual abundance, and grace after mental illness.

In fact, let us look at it another way; perhaps a mental breakdown is not a mental breakdown. Perhaps it is simply you coming to the end of your human mental strength and capabilities and experiencing the beginning of God's supernatural intervention. Look at it as a new time filled with second chances and new mercies. A time of reflection, rest, renewal, awakening and rebirth. A chance to put away the old ways of being or thinking that were causing so much mental pain and sadness and building new ways of living and thinking.

The good news is, this time, you will not lean on your own strength or your own knowledge and understanding. This time you will let the grace of God and The Holy Spirit of God be your comfort and guide while you renew and rebuild your mind and life. God's strength is sufficient, especially in our weaknesses (6). We were never meant to live this life apart from God and his power.

During your time (of mental renewal) it is not about what you can or cannot do or control, but it is about doing everything in God's strength. Renewing your mind is a life-long journey and with patience, practice, and prayer a renewed mind is possible.

Beloved, let me start by admitting that I was not raised to know how to think wonderful, righteous thoughts. I was not taught that my thoughts and beliefs should always be good because they dictate how I view myself and the world. Because of this (having an unguarded mind) I believed whatever anyone told me, and I developed (in my mind) a negative, self-destructive, self-defeating image of who I was and my place in this world. Being a darker skinned black girl growing up in the projects in the 1980's and having no sense of self, direction or purpose lead me down a path of disaster. This path ultimately led to my mental breakdown at the age of 34.

All the knowledge and information I include in this book about guarding, renewing, and rebuilding your mind was gained by personal experience, living through 25 years of trials, mental illness, hardships, and 15 years of intense therapy. During my stay in the mental hospital, I spoke open and honestly to God. It had become evident that my old negative habits, and toxic ways of thinking and behaving had gotten me to this place of complete mental breakdown (some of my thoughts and behaviors were simply defense mechanisms I had built up to protect myself from a society that believed because I was a Black Female I was worthy of nothing good and decent and I could achieve nothing more than being the mother of some children, collecting a welfare check, and dying of some preventable disease). I would be lying to you if I told you that I did not believe those lies to some degree. (When you see these very things happening to most of the women around you, you tend to believe that no matter how hard you try, this just may be your fate as well.) After many years of living a self-destructive lifestyle, I found myself in the hospital suffering from a mental breakdown. I knew it was time for a change or else I would die prematurely and leave my children without a mother. I needed to transform my life (with the help of God) and the way to do that was to renew my mind. So right there in the hospital, I asked God to heal my mind, my heart, and my soul. I asked him to show me how to live victoriously, give me the strength to finish raising my children, and be the woman I knew he had created me to be and was calling me to be. In exchange for my deliverance and mental healing I promised God that I would help others by bringing awareness to the origins of mental illness and I would help them to receive his light and truth into their minds and hearts. This book was written as a small part of my thanks to God for leading me out of the dark places of my mind into his wonderful light. I pray that this book will be a light and a glimmer of hope to all of those who read it. Especially to those of you who may find yourself swept away by the negative raging thoughts of your mind and are fighting every day to find peace. I want you to know you are not alone. I want you to know that you are not meant to live in your mistakes but to learn from them so they will not be repeated. You do not have to carry negative experiences and thoughts around in your mind. God loves you and cares about what you go through. Through Him, you are courageous, strong, smart, and brilliant just as you are, right where you are! You were created to be a wonderfully beautiful reflection of God's grace and to have a mind that is healthy and strong.

"The most beautiful people we have known are those who have known defeat, known suffering, known struggle, known loss, and have found their way out of those depths. These persons have an appreciation, a sensitivity, and an understanding of life that fills them with compassion, gentleness, and a deep loving concern. Beautiful people do not just happen."

-Elizabeth Kubler Ross.

Part 1

MENTAL HEALTH

Chapter 1

The Mind

Casting down imaginations, and every high thing that exalts itself against the knowledge of God and bringing into captivity every thought to the obedience of Christ (1).

The oxford dictionary (2020) defines the mind as "the element of a person that enables them to be aware of the world and their experiences, to think, and to feel: the faculty of consciousness and thought" (2). This definition shows us that the condition of our mind and our mental state play a very important role in our everyday life. Our minds and thoughts ultimately decide how we will live and function from day to day. For this reason, we cannot afford to let our minds stop working properly, break down, or become diseased. Knowing how to guard our mind is so important. Guarding our mind is the first line of defense against lies and bad thoughts because the mind is the first place the devil will attack with his lies and deception. We will talk more about what it will take to keep our minds and hearts guarded in Chapter 4 of Part 1.

God promised to keep us in perfect peace if we keep our minds on (continually meditate on) him (3). Through my own personal experience and listening to other testimonies, it has become clear to me that a mind apart from God (the holy spirit), prayer, and his word is not a well-guarded mind and is highly susceptible to the attacks and lies of Satan and other evil people we may encounter in our daily lives. Meaning that - to experience superior mental health - you must establish and maintain a personal relationship with God (the creator). A relationship with God that is filled with thanksgiving and gratitude, time spent in his word and fervent prayer. Living a Godly life is not only about sitting in a pew on Saturday or Sunday mornings, but it is about what we say, think, and do every other day of the week.

In the years leading up to my emotional and mental breakdown, my relationship with God had been severed by my lack of desire for him and his presence. I desired the things of the world more than I desired the things of God. I desired to be accepted by man more than I wanted to be accepted by God. I also valued and feared the worlds approval and opinion of me and my life more than God's. My soul was disconnected from its power source and because of this I unknowingly set myself up for a mental, spiritual, emotional, and physical death (I say physical death because during this time I also became a heavy drug user). Having a personal relationship with Christ is critical to maintaining your mental health and living a peaceful, prosperous life. I would even venture to say that they cannot exist apart from each other. A life without God is like a vehicle without gasoline. You can clean the car every Sunday and give it a good wax but without that gasoline in the tank it will not get you anywhere.

Unfortunately, we do not think about our minds, our thoughts, or our mental health until we (or a loved one) encounter a mental crisis. This is when we usually hear the words "Depression" "Anxiety" or "Bi-polar." Now, whether these words are being used to describe our mental state or the mental state of a family member or friend, they lead us to further explore the subject of mental health. Part 1 of this book will show you how to prevent your mind from falling into the mental traps that are designed to destroy your peace of mind and disrupt your life. These mind traps cause our minds to become susceptible to mental diseases such as bi-polar, depression, anxiety, and psychosis; all of which are diseases of the mind. Disease of any kind, when left unchecked, will turn into an illness and chronic illness often leads to death.

In the Beginning

To give you a better understanding of just how important and sacred the human mind and thoughts are we will go back to the garden of Eden. In the third book of Genesis, we find Eve (the first woman created by the hand of God) in the garden talking to a serpent (that had been over-taken by the spirit of Satan) (4). Satan makes his purpose very clear; he wanted access to her mind. He already knew that her mind was filled with good knowledge, but he wanted the ability to plant bad (or evil) knowledge and thoughts into her mind (5). Satan tells Eve that she will not die, although God had already told Adam that anyone who ate the fruit off the tree in the middle of the garden would die (6). Satan lied to (deceived) Eve about what would happen if she disobeyed God and ate the fruit of the forbidden tree. Genesis 3:5, KJV says (Satan is speaking to Eve) "for God knows that in the day ye eat thereof that your eyes shall be open, and ye shall be as gods, knowing good and evil. This scripture lets us know that the only knowledge Adam and Eve had in their minds up to this point was good, wholesome knowledge. Satan tells Eve that eating the apple will give her access to bad (or evil) knowledge as well as the good and he sweetens his proposal by saying that they shall also be as god's (knowing good and evil). Satan knew that the human mind was not equipped to handle this evil knowledge. However, Eve's single act of disobedience gave Satan a way to download evil, negative, self-destructive thoughts into her mind and the minds of all human beings, including those of us alive today. Satan knew that by having this access he could destroy us from within and with little effort. After Eve's act of disobedience, the mind of mankind became a battle ground between good and evil. The Holy Spirit and the word of God are the first lines of defense against the lies of the enemy. (To learn more about the whole armor of God see Ephesians 6:11).

What were the first bad thoughts and emotions (evil knowledge) planted in the mind of Adam and Eve? The first (evil) thought Satan planted in their mind's was designed to attack and distort Adam and Eve's self-image and self-perception. The first evil thing they thought after eating the apple was that something was very wrong with who they were and how God had made them: They realized that they were naked! (7) Although it is noted in the previous chapter that the man and woman knew they were naked and were NOT ashamed (8). The act of disobedience by Eve (eating the apple) not only gave Satan the ability to plant evil knowledge into their minds but it gave him the ability to turn good knowledge into evil knowledge (or truth into lies). He turned their awareness of being naked from something that they were okay with, something that previously had no effect on them, into something bad and shameful.

There are feelings that are attached to every thought (good or bad) we think. The feelings of shame and fear were attached to the first negative thoughts (or evil knowledge) to enter the minds of Adam and Eve after their act of disobedience (9)." Satan told Eve she would be able to have access to this evil knowledge once she ate the apple. What he failed to mention is that having evil knowledge in your mind will cause your mind to become diseased, which will cause you to behave poorly. He (Satan) knew that it would be easier to control people by having access to their minds. When information is coming from within (our minds) we think it has come from us but from this day on I want you to realize that evil knowledge and thoughts come directly from Satan, and you must rebuke them as soon as they enter your mind. The first thing he (Satan) did was plant (evil) knowledge in their minds. Knowledge that would make them feel fearful, shameful, and anxious enough separate themselves from God. He knew that to finish destroying them he would first have to separate them from God's protection and provisions. (Doesn't it seem Satan is still up to his same old tricks today? Distorting our perceptions of ourselves by planting negative thoughts.)

Adam and Eve's new feelings of shame, fear, and dread caused them to behave in an unusual way. (Our thoughts produce our feelings, and our feelings dictate our behavior). The negative feelings made them hide (or run) from their creator. Unfortunately, the feelings of shame and fear still have the same effect today. The evil knowledge (which was the awareness that being naked was now a very bad thing) produced feelings of dread, fear, and shame which caused them to separate themselves from their creator. The same creator who was aware of their nakedness because he had made them that way and was very pleased with who they were and how they were made. It is important to note that sin and disobedience still have the same affect today as it did back then. It separates us from God, gives Satan direct access to our lives, and puts our souls on the path to destruction.

The feelings of shame, fear, embarrassment, and humiliation were attached to the evil new knowledge. You can most often identify evil thoughts, knowledge, and information because they will always produce evil (bad or negative) feelings and emotions. Adam and Eve's spiritual war started in their minds! Satan was able to make them think something was wrong with who they were. Not only did they think this, but they believed it and acted upon this thought (this lie). It is important to note that any act of disobedience to God opens us up to mental, physical, and emotional attacks from the enemy of our souls. It is better to obey God and remain at peace both mentally and spiritually. Obedience begins in the mind and then the heart. Obedience brings blessings and disobedience brings curses. It is very wise to obey God, it will keep your mind at peace.

Perhaps, just like Adam and Eve, you have a distorted or negative self-image. you have believed the lies of evil people who have told you that you are worthless, useless, and dumb. Now you have a constant feeling that something is wrong with who you are and how God made you. If this is the case, over time you can retrain your mind to see yourself as God sees you: fearfully and wonderfully made in His image (10). You can turn negative self-defeating thinking around by renewing your mind. You must not let sin or bad, negative feelings and emotions make you run from God or hide from God. Instead, go boldly to His throne of grace (through prayer) where you can obtain mercy and find the grace to help you (defeat these negative thoughts) in your time of need (11).

Over time you will learn to love yourself as God loves you and see yourself as God sees you: both precious and priceless. Whenever your mind begins to produce self-defeating thoughts keep repeating the following scripture (if you can, say it out loud): "I will praise thee, for I am fearfully and wonderfully made, marvelous are thy works, and that my soul knows right well" (12). Say this to yourself as often as necessary. You will find that over time you will begin to see yourself and treat yourself as the beautiful, courageous, majestic human being that God created you to be.

There is a section in the back of this book loaded with scriptures that will help you maintain your mental health and make your mind (and life) a place of peace. In Chapter 4 of part 1, I will talk more about how to combat the lies and negative thoughts planted in our minds by the enemy of our souls (Satan).

Scripture (the word of God) will always be the main weapon in defeating Satan's lies. The word of God is referred to as the sword of the spirit because it can cut through and kill the lies of the enemy in both spiritual and mental warfare (13). God's word will keep lies and negative thoughts from growing in the garden of your mind, causing you mental distress, and preventing you from growing both spiritually and mentally.

One more important thing to note about the fall of man in the Garden of Eden is the way in which God compared disobedience and knowing how to think evil thoughts to death. God told Adam that the day he ate of the fruit he would surely die (14). The type of death God was referring to when he told Adam he would surely die if he did eat of the forbidden fruit was a not a physical death but a spiritual and mental death. We know this because after eating the fruit Adam and Eve did not physically die. However, they were driven out of the garden (separated from Gods provisions, protection, and goodness) to work by the sweat of their brow (15). Adam and Eve's act of disobedience caused them to die both spiritually and mentally. Now not only were they separated from God (their source of life) they also had a mind filled with evil knowledge. They now had to figure out how to mentally separate the evil knowledge from good knowledge. They also had to decipher which thoughts were from God and which thoughts were from Satan. They had to do this while learning how to provide for themselves and their children for the first time. This marked the beginning of the battle of the mind.

Beloved the condition of your mind is important. Your mental health is important. Feed your mind good thoughts just like you feed your body good, healthy food. If you understand that you should not drink or eat anything harmful or poisonous, then you should not allow your mind to think or believe harmful or poisonous thoughts. Always think good thoughts and when your life and circumstances look bleak and unbearable do not begin to let sadness and doubt creep in. Begin walking by faith and not by sight. (16).

Maintaining Emotions

Developing a mind that is your place of joy and peace takes patience and practice. You will not get it right every day. You will get angry, but you must not let your anger drive you to sin (17). Yes, we are allowed and even equipped to feel emotions such as anger, fear, sadness, disappointment, hurt, and frustration. It is what we choose to do with these emotions that will determine whether we continue to live in victory and joy or live in a state of bitterness, bondage, and fear. Learning how to control your thoughts and emotions will set you up for success in every area of your life. Self-control is a broad topic, but we will look at it from a mental health perspective. If you do not want to be dragged around by your emotions, you will need self-control.

With so many things seeming to be out of our control especially at a young age, (things like the family and neighborhood we are born into and raised in, the schools and friends we meet along the way) it is a must that we learn to control ourselves and the thoughts that we let enter our minds. To do this, you must, according to the wisdom of King Solomon, get an understanding (18). First understand that no matter what is going on around you, no matter what others think about you, that you, just like every other human being was created by the Almighty God and that you are a beautiful reflection of his grace, goodness, and mercy. Your existence on this earth has meaning and purpose, no matter where you live or what you look like.

When bad things happen to you at a young age (like they did to me) you must understand that what happens to you does not define you. Yes, it may hurt you deeply, (it is okay to acknowledge that hurt and pain) but it should not (must not) stop you from becoming the purposeful, radiant, kind, loving human being God created you to be. Satan starts working very early to inflict pain on human beings. This is because when we are young our minds are still forming and often unable to understand pain and suffering. Often when young people are hurt, they take on the feelings associated with the hurt and pain and make those feelings their identity. But you are not defeated. You are not damaged. You are victorious. You are a survivor. And you will grow up to do amazing things and when you truly believe these things in your mind, you have already started to win the battle of the mind.

CHAPTER 1 PRAYER POINT:

Father God, I thank you for my mind, I thank you for the ability to think, to feel and to create wonderful thoughts and ideas with my mind. I consecrate my mind and I ask you to help me guard my mind from evil knowledge and negative information. Give me the strength and discernment to always choose the right thoughts and to get rid of all evil thoughts and information. In Jesus name I pray, ask, and believe. Amen.

Chapter 2

A Healthy Mind

> (1) Blessed is the man that walks not in the counsel of the ungodly, nor stands in the way of sinners, nor sits in the seat of the scornful. (2) But his delight is in the law of the Lord and in this law, he meditates day and night. (1).

Since God is the one who designed us, there lies within each of us a spirit, soul, and mind that can only be sustained by being closely connected to God through the Holy Spirit (2). Maintaining a close connection with God will ensure that our thoughts are aligned with his word. Being spiritually minded is life and peace (3). Being spiritually minded also attracts the blessings and favor of God because when your mind is at peace your life will be blessed and fruitful.

In the book of Psalms, King David describes the life of someone who meditates on (thinks on) God's word day and night. King David opens the book of Psalms by declaring

“Blessed is the man that walks not in the counsel of the ungodly, nor stands in the way with sinners, nor sits in the seat of the scornful, but his delight is in the law of the Lord and in this law, he meditates day and night (4). To meditate means to think deeply or carefully about something (Oxford Dictionary, 2020).

In this opening scripture King David is clear about the things a person should do to be considered blessed. The first thing we see is that: The blessed individual does not take advice or counsel from the ungodly- meaning that when you need advice you should not get it from a friend or family member who does not have their own personal relationship with Christ. In verse 2: (The blessed individual) does not stand in the way with sinners – meaning that other than witnessing Christ to sinners and unbelievers a blessed Christian will make every attempt to be separated from sinners and sin. In verse 3: (The blessed individual) does not sit in the seat eat of the scornful. The seat of the scornful is usually occupied by bitter, prideful, high-minded individuals. A scornful individual intentionally seeks to condemn and judge others. Since Christ has called us to love ourselves and one another a blessed individual does not scorn others but privately and lovingly helps them to see their sin or wrong-doing and offers counsel on how to be better. However, to scorn a person or be scornful is done to intentionally cause public shame, embarrassment, humiliation, and intimidation, all of which are not attributes of Christ. Scornful people are not blessed people according to this scripture. The heart and mind of a scornful person lacks peace and joy and is usually filled with anger, hatred, and resentment.

The second verse of Psalms chapter 1 is what I want to call your attention to. This verse tells us what the blessed individual (you and me) should be thinking about or meditating on day and night. It states that the Bible (law of God) is what the blessed individual should be meditating on day and night. The Bible is a life manual and a road map, if you read it and apply its principles to your life, you will always arrive at your divine destination and live the abundant, prosperous life that God wants you to live. It is not enough to just memorize scripture or read the bible, you must apply it to your life like you would apply ointment to a wound. The word of God is only affective when you apply its Biblical principles to your daily life. Meaning that - you should not only read the scriptures, but you must also practice them as well.

The blessed individual that King David speaks about in Psalms chapter 1 does certain things to maintain their blessed life. King David continues speaking about this blessed individual, saying "but his delight is in the law of the Lord, and in this law does he meditate day and night (6). I want you to focus on the word meditate. Meditation is something that can only take place in the mind and heart. As stated above, it means to think deeply or intensely about something. To meditate on God's word, you must first read it, then you must think deeply about it; ponder it both day and night. This does not mean you have to walk around with a bible attached to your hip. You can read a scripture in the morning that you meditate on throughout your day. Just be sure to get the word of God into your mind every day. It will be a shield for your mind, helping you keep evil information and knowledge out of your mind, and maintain your mental health.

The mind is like a garden and meditating on God's word will ensure that the soil in the garden of your mind remains fresh, fertile, and ready to receive good seeds (or thoughts). It also will ensure that only the seeds (or thoughts) that align with the word of God are able to take root and grow. Remember, the blessed individual King David describes delights themselves in the law of the Lord which is the word of God. King David says that not only does this blessed individual delight themselves in the law of the Lord, but they meditate on (or think deeply about) this law both day and night.

In this Chapter you have been given some important information pertaining to the mind and how our thoughts manifest into behaviors. I have simplified the information in this chapter by breaking it down into 5 key points that I really want you to understand. To maintain a healthy mind and a blessed life you:

Point 1. Meditate on (thinking intensely about) the law of God (the word of God) day and night. Before reading the word of God, pray and ask God to help you apply the word to your heart, mind, and life as you go through your day. You do not want to just read the word of God, but you want to obey it as well.

Point 2. Do not take advice or counsel from ungodly or unwise people. If you are given advice from ungodly family or friends, ask God for discernment regarding this advice. If you need therapy or counseling, try to seek out a Christian counselor who incorporates the word of God and prayer in their counseling sessions.

Point 3. Do not keep company with sinners who willfully and openly sin. Separate yourself from sinful friends and family. Pray and ask God for godly, wise friends and mentors. Sometimes life will require you to walk alone for a season. Do not despise the season of solitude and isolation. Even Jesus had his season of isolation in the wilderness. Choose to be by yourself instead of being with sinners who will lead you into sin and mischief. God is preparing you for something greater during these times.

Point 4. Do not be a scornful person (remember to scorn means to maliciously remind others of their faults and shortcomings with the intention of causing them to feel shame and humiliation). You will find that a scornful person is operating out of a spirit of bitterness which is not a fruit of the spirit given by God. Do all things with love, kindness, and compassion.

Point 5: Be patient with yourself. Meditating on anything day and night takes discipline, practice, and patience. Be gentle with yourself. Try your very best to carve out time in the morning and at night to read the Bible. If you want to maintain superior mental health and live a blessed life you will have to find time for the word of God. Practice makes perfect.

I encourage you to read Psalms Chapter 1 in its entirety. King David does a phenomenal job describing the life of a blessed individual and the benefits of being a blessed individual. For example, verse 3 of Psalms Chapter 1 describes some of the blessings that will follow the individual who mediates on the law of the Lord both day and night. Verse 3 (Psalms chapter 1) states that the blessed individual who meditates on the law of the Lord will be like a tree bearing good fruit in a good season. The best part of verse 3 is the ending which states that (because this blessed individual meditates on the law of the Lord) whatsoever they do will prosper! Can you imagine that? Meditate on that wonderful news for a moment! Whatever I do will prosper if I can learn to apply the simple principles King David mentioned in Psalms 1:1-2? Yes, and that is very good news! That means starting your business will prosper, starting your ministry will prosper and your efforts to maintain your mental health will prosper. The word whatsoever means just that! It means whatever you do will prosper. If it is in line with the will and word of God for your life, it will prosper!

CHAPTER 2 PRAYER POINT:

Father God, we thank you for your word and that you have taught us through your word how to keep our minds healthy and sound. We pray for a deeper understanding of your word, a desire to read your word both day and night and to apply it to our hearts and minds. We seek, through your word, to develop healthy thinking patterns that will enable us to live an abundant life, love ourselves, and dwell peacefully with others. Grant us these desires in Jesus' name. Amen

Chapter 3

Maintaining Your Mental Health

> Finally, beloved, whatsoever things are true, whatsoever things are honest, whatsoever things are just, whatsoever things are pure, whatsoever things are lovely, whatsoever things are of good report, if there be any virtue, if there be any praise, think on these things (1).

Thoughts Produce Feelings and Behavior

When you grow up not learning how to guard your mind you will unknowingly (by default) let unhealthy, toxic thoughts (seeds) grow in the garden of your mind. My first unhealthy thought was that my dad left my mom because I was not good enough. I not only thought this, but I believed (in my young mind) that my dad looked at me and said she is not good enough to be my daughter and he left my mom. Over time this negative, false thought began to grow and produce negative feelings and emotions (remember that our thoughts produce feelings, and those feelings dictate out behavior). The lie along with the feelings it produced, went unchecked, causing me to have a poor self-image and an unhealthy belief about myself that produced the feelings of shame, fear, anxiety, abandonment, and low self-esteem (the same feelings Adam and Eve felt in the garden). These feelings drove me away from God and down a very dark path at an early age. I became needy for any man's attention and acceptance because it was how I measured my worth and value. Having this kind of mentality caused me to become trapped in sexual promiscuity and prostitution at 14 years old, followed by drug addiction and homosexuality at 17 years old. All of this happened because I believed (in my young mind) the lie (or thought) that I was not good enough for my dad and would never be good enough for anyone else.

I held on to the lie (or negative thought) in my mind that I was not good enough until I was 19 years old. (The actual truth was that my father was a drug-addicted alcoholic who had been abandoned by his father. My father had his own demons that drove him into a life of alcoholism, drug addiction and caused him to choose these things over being a father to his children. This addiction led to his death in 2011). A couple years before my father's death (when I was 28 years-old and had already given birth to my two children) he apologized for not being the father that I needed him to be. God had healed that situation.

Nevertheless, I had spent most of my childhood and young adulthood trying to rationalize the absence of my father, and because no explanation was given, I rationalized it by thinking (and believing) that he was gone because something was bad or wrong with me (not him). This bad thought is an example of a bad seed that was planted in the garden of my mind at an early age. This thought began producing feelings of fear, anxiety, sadness, and low self-worth. These negative feelings led me to indulge in more self-destructive thoughts and behaviors.

Unhealthy thoughts that we allow to grow in the garden of our minds will ultimately lead to unhealthy feelings and emotions, these unhealthy feelings and emotions will lead to an unhealthy self-image and having an unhealthy self-image will cause us to make unhealthy choices. Constantly making poor decisions and unhealthy choices will cause mental distress and disease. When our minds become diseased, we will begin to behave in ways that reflect the disease and turmoil in our minds.

Taking care of the garden of your mind (or maintaining your mental health) involves paying close attention to the thoughts that you allow to enter your mind. If these thoughts are bad (or produce feelings that are bad) and contrary to the word of God, do not allow these thoughts to take root and grow in the soil of your mind. Rebuke and ignore them immediately. Doing this immediately is important because once bad, negative, stinky thoughts begin to grow in the garden of your mind they will produce feelings of shame, fear, anxiety, guilt, depression, loneliness, anger, impatience, self-hatred, and extreme sadness. These feelings will contaminate the garden of your mind if they go unchecked and cause you to behave in a shameful, fearful, anxious manner. Eventually, your mind will become ill, and you will start to experience feelings like extreme sadness, depression, impulsivity, and anger.

Once your mind becomes diseased or you encounter a mental crisis, you cannot escape your mind or receive a mind transplant. Therefore, knowing how to guard your mind from lies, and toxic thoughts is extremely important. I have said this before, but it is worth repeating; just as consuming bad, toxic foods will cause you to become physically ill, consuming bad, toxic thoughts, beliefs and knowledge will cause you to become mentally and emotionally ill.

Remember that you must take your mind with you wherever you go. If your heart, lungs, or kidneys are diseased you may be able to receive a transplant. If your mind is diseased or becomes ill you will have to figure out how to recalibrate, readjust and renew your mind. This cannot be done by your own might, or by your own power but by the spirit of God (2). I know because I have had to do it. For 26 years I continually allowed toxic thoughts into my mind (even making them my truth) and built relationships with people who (I knew) were toxic. I did not guard my mind or heart because I did not know how. (I will talk more about how to renew your mind in part three of this book).

Beloved, remember you have the power over your mind. You must give your consent for thoughts to be planted in your mind and you must give consent for them to grow there. You water or give life to a bad thought (seed) and allow it to grow when you constantly think about it, or refuse to acknowledge it, heal it, and let it go.

In our childhood and young adult years we are surrounded by family and our environment. Some of us are not as fortunate as others. Some of us must grow up in a family filled with verbally, physically, and mentally toxic, violent, abusive people. We must grow up in drug infested, crime ridden neighborhoods. Being in these types of environments make us more likely to encounter negative people, thoughts, feelings, and emotions. Satan will use negative situations, such as being raised in poverty, to get you to start thinking and believing that something is wrong with you and that you have been forgotten by God. If you are being (or have been) raised in a toxic, abusive family that makes (or made) you feel sad, depressed, unloved, and unsafe please know that you are not alone. I was raised in similar circumstances. Here is what I want you to do:

First, whenever possible find some alone time, and in this alone time talk open and honestly to God (he is always listening). Ask him to fill your heart with the peace, love, and safety that you cannot (or could not) find in your family or community. He will! Secondly, whenever possible read many books (including the Bible). Fill your mind with good news, knowledge, and information. Your mind is your sacred space. A space in which you can retreat to when chaos is all around you. When you fill your mind with prayer, good knowledge, and good thoughts it will be a place of peace and stillness. Read the bible and read books that challenge you to use your imagination in a healthy positive way. Thirdly, (and this third thing may take some time and may not happen until you become an adult and separate yourself from your toxic family and environment) forgive those who caused you pain as a child and young adult.

Your parents, caregivers, uncles, and aunts may not have done everything right but perhaps their mind was diseased, and they quietly suffered from a form of mental illness while trying to give you the best life they possibly could. You may not be able to forgive as quickly as Jesus forgave his murders while he was dying on the cross but ask God daily for the spirit of forgiveness (3). He will answer you and give you the strength and courage to truly forgive all those who have wronged you.

Forgiveness is a daily choice. It is also a mind and heart exercise. It will strengthen your heart and free you from walking in bitterness and anger. Jesus tells us to forgive quickly because holding on to unforgiveness and the thoughts associated with it will produce feelings of bitterness, anger, and resentment. Having these negative feelings in your heart and mind will make it impossible for the seeds of joy, peace, and righteousness to take root and grow (4). If you had a childhood filled with abusive, toxic, and neglectful adults, forgive them, and never believe that you are worthless, bad, dirty, or unimportant because of the abuse you suffered at the hands of those you trusted. You are not your circumstances, experiences, or environment. You do not have to become an abusive, dysfunctional adult because all the adults in your life were. Also, if the young men and women in your neighborhood or environment are having sex and doing drugs, you do not have to copy them. You can make up in your mind that you will live your life differently. (Do not talk badly about, look down upon, or scorn those who have made and continue to make bad choices, instead pray sincerely for them).

Again, your mind is your sacred space, and in your mind, you must always view yourself as good, smart, strong, brave, and important. Even if your peers, family, or other outside sources try to make you believe something different. I have found, through my own personal experience and through hearing the testimonies of other people who grew up in abusive and toxic environments, that beginnings such as these are reserved for people who usually turn out to be dynamic leaders, thinkers, and innovators. Adversity strengthens us and our messy beginnings become our testimonies of strength and survival later in life. Just as God was with Moses, abandoned by his Hebrew mother as an infant, God will be with you. (5). God will use your beginning that may have been marred by abandonment and rejection, like Moses's was, and raise you up to be a great leader doing the greater works (6).

Your painful beginning does not mean you will have a painful ending. Although you might be surrounded by negativity your mind is your secret place. Your mind and imagination have been given to you by God as places in which you can hide out and plan your vision for a better life or just simply talk to and be with God. Recall the story of Cinderella. She was treated as a servant in her own home by her family. Yet in her alone time she envisioned a life of wonder and amazement. She did this every day. She refused to let her circumstances make her bitter, mean, angry and sad. Every day she imagined and envisioned a better life. The story of Cinderella ends better than she had imagined every day all those years earlier. The prince asked for her hand in marriage, and she enjoyed a life living in the castle with her own servants serving her for the rest of her life. Whatever you envision for your future, write it out. Make your vision a big one so that God can exceed your expectations.

What are Right Thoughts?

The Apostle Paul wrote a letter to the beloved Church in Philippi. His letters were written to guide, uplift, admonish, encourage, and fortify the new and old believers there. In Paul's letter to the Philippian Church, he tells them what right thoughts are and that these are the only thoughts they should be thinking. Paul says "Finally, brethren (brothers and sisters), whatsoever things are true, whatsoever things are honest, whatsoever things are just, whatsoever things are pure, whatsoever things are lovely, whatsoever things are of good report, if there be any virtue, if there be any praise, think on these things (7).

So, what are right thoughts? Right thoughts consist of ones that will produce right (or good) feelings. Feelings of joy, peace, and love. Right thoughts make you feel warm and safe. You will also be able to identify these right thoughts because of the good fruit (or behaviors) they produce once they have been planted and begin to grow in the soil of your mind. These good fruits are also known as spiritual fruit, and they grow in so much abundance and goodness that when you share them with others, they will also be able to feel love, joy, and peace. The fruits of the spirit (that begin to grow in the garden of your mind when you think good thoughts) are love, joy, peace, long-suffering, gentleness, goodness, faith, meekness, and temperance (or self-control) (8). Good thoughts always produce good things (emotions, feelings, and behaviors) as well. For example, when you think you are courageous and brave you will feel energetic, happy, and motivated to do great things. When you think you are useless and unimportant you will feel depressed, sad, and fearful about doing everything. When our thoughts are good and pure our actions will be as well.

Have you ever met a person who was so full of joy and peace, they were very nice to you, and gave you a smile, a hug, or a gift? This is because their mind (or thoughts) produced feelings of joy, peace and gratitude and other people benefit from their good, positive thinking (your behavior will reflect your thoughts). Now let us look at this another way. Have you ever run into a very mean, nasty, bitter person who scorned you and made you feel bad? They act that way because they have a mind and heart that produces the negative fruits (thoughts and feelings) of bitterness and anger. Whatever is in a person's heart and mind is all they can present to others. Our mind is the place we pull everything from when we interact with the world. If, in your mind you are insecure and have a negative self-image then you will present yourself to the world as an insecure, needy individual. Mean and insecure people have diseased minds and are often the source of nasty words and lies. They are quick to belittle and demean others. The saddest part of the life of a person who is living with a diseased mind is that not only do they interact with others in a diseased way, but they are also often very self-critical and self-sabotaging as well. Meaning that they also treat themselves poorly. Again, knowing how to guard your mind and maintain your mental health is essential if you wish to live a blessed life filled with peace and joy. If you wish to be an effective witness and example of the love of Jesus in this life you must have the mind of Christ (9). You will need the proper gardening tools to keep the garden of your mind blooming beautifully, producing the fruits (thoughts) that taste good to other people, and add value to your life and the Kingdom of God.

What are Wrong Thoughts?

Like eating bad food will make you physically ill, thinking the wrong thoughts will, over-time, make you mentally ill. So, what are wrong thoughts? They are the opposite of right thoughts and will most always produce negative feelings and emotions and cause you to behave in a negative way. Wrong thoughts are when we start thinking things like, *I am unworthy, disgusting, and dirty.* Wrong thoughts produce feelings of low self-worth, depression, anxiety, shame, and anger. These feelings fester in our hearts and minds and cause us to behave in negative ways. The negative behavior reflects the negative thoughts and feelings. When you see someone battling with a mental illness or addictions it is often because they have let negative experiences, thoughts, and feelings linger in their mind and heart too long. Allowing negative thoughts and experiences along with the feelings they produce stay in the mind for long periods of time will create dis-ease and when there is a disease of the mind it will manifest through negative behaviors. When people think badly about themselves, they often treat themselves and others badly. Again, wrong thoughts always produce wrong or bad feelings and behaviors. Let us look at some wrong thoughts and the feelings and behaviors they can produce:

Thoughts	Feelings and Behavior
I am worthless	Low self-esteem, anxiety / addictions to food, drugs, toxic people.
I am not smart	Depression, hopelessness/ unproductivity, and lack of motivation.
I cannot do this	Fear, anxiety/ Lack of vision or goals for life, no achievement or growth.
I am too scared to	Hopelessness, poverty, fear/ addictions, bad choices.
No one loves me	Depression, loneliness, sadness/ addictions, and bad choices.

CHAPTER 3 PRAYER POINT:

Father God, I thank you for my mind and I thank you for my life. I ask that you have patience with me, strengthen me, and show me how to renew my mind and fill it with good thoughts. I believe that you are the eternal God, and it is my desire to have a mind that produces thoughts that reflect your grace and goodness. I pray for a mind that produces thoughts that are good enough to share with and encourage others. I love you and I ask these things in Jesus' name. Amen

Chapter 4

The Garden of Your Mind

> It is like a grain of a mustard seed, which a man took, and cast into his garden, and it grew into a great tree, and the fowls of the air lodged in the branches of it (1).

The Garden of Your Mind

Maintaining the garden of your mind and your mental health is up to you. Yes, bad knowledge can find its way into our minds but through the word of God, the holy spirit, and daily prayer we can gain the strength to denounce and reject these bad thoughts and replace them with good thoughts. Being equipped with the proper tools will make you a master gardener in the garden of your mind.

The garden of your mind will be a thing of beauty and admiration. Others will be encouraged by the thoughts that you think and love hearing what you have to say. In this chapter we will discuss some essential gardening tools that you will need to maintain your mental health and keep the garden of your mind healthy. When it is time to harvest all the wonderful thoughts that you have carefully planted, cultivated, and grown in your mind garden, you will reap a bountiful harvest that will be good enough to share with everyone you meet.

First, the soil in your mind (garden) must be fertile and ready to receive and nourish the righteous seeds that are planted in it every day. In the bible Jesus refers to it as being "good ground" (2). Keeping the soil of your mind ready to receive and grow good seeds requires tilling. To till means to prepare and cultivate (Oxford Dictionary 2020). Cultivating the soil in your mind garden will make it good ground that is ready to receive good seeds (or good news, knowledge, and information). For example, someone can tell you that you are beautiful, strong, and brave but if the soil of your mind is hard or stony (meaning it is still holding on to and growing thoughts of self-doubt and low self-worth) the good information has no room to grow. Whatever seed you allow to be planted is exactly what will grow. A good seed or thought produces good fruit, and a bad seed or thought will produce bad fruit. The tool you will use to till the soil in your mind garden, preparing it to receive good thoughts is prayer coupled with patience.

In the letter written by the Apostle's Paul, Silvanus, and Timothy to the church located in Thessalonica, the Apostle's gave the believer's specific instructions to: Rejoice evermore, pray without ceasing, and in everything give thanks, for this is the will of God in Christ Jesus concerning you (4). I will tell you that if you put these three things (rejoice, pray, and give thanks) into practice every day you will start to see that the garden of your mind and your life will be a place of joy and peace. Your thoughts and actions will begin to reflect this joy and peace and you will be a pleasure to be around. You will find yourself doing less complaining and more rejoicing. To put this in biblical terms: you will become a good tree bearing good fruit (5).

I suggest that your main prayer times takes place right after you open your eyes in the morning and before you go to sleep at night. These two prayer times are more likely to be filled with gratitude and thanksgiving. Communicate with God throughout your day; before you get ready for class or make that cup of coffee, before you go to that job that you love or hate, before you get ready to speak to your child out of anger, or while you are taking your morning walk. Prayer can be done at any time and in any place because it takes place in your mind and heart.

Praying throughout your day will condition and cultivate the soil of your mind preparing it to receive and nourish healthy thoughts. Having a constant attitude of thanksgiving and gratitude will also help cultivate and prepare your life to receive the blessings of God. Find things (big or small) throughout your day to be thankful for and make this a daily practice. The Apostle's Paul, Silvanus, and Timotheus directed the members of the church at Thessalonica to give thanks in all things, for this is the will of God in Christ Jesus concerning them (6). Be mindful of all the wonderful things you have to be thankful for. If possible, write them down, even if it is simply the fact that you are breathing and alive. Give thanks in and for all things.

Now that your soil has been tilled and prepared to receive good thoughts (seeds) you need to be able to immediately identify good thoughts, good people, good experiences, good words, and good works. Having the ability to do this properly is called discernment. Discernment is defined as the ability to judge well (Oxford Languages Dictionary, 2020). The garden tool of discernment will be your seed sorter. Use this tool to help you to sort the bad seeds (thoughts) from the good seeds (thoughts) and bad people from good people. Asking God through prayer for wisdom and the spirit of discernment is the first step to receiving it. Then you must activate it by using it whenever you are presented with different thoughts, experiences, and feelings. Remember, some thoughts are just so bad that they are never supposed to be planted in the garden of your mind.

You must judge all things well to keep contaminated thoughts out of your garden and to maintain mental peace and clarity. For example, when words of hatred and bitterness are presented to you from an outside source (maybe a friend, co-worker, or family member), these words meet your ear and enter your mind, they suggest you may not be as smart or as good as other people. What do you do with these words you have just heard? First, let us look at the feelings they produce then you will know whether these words should be planted in the garden of your mind or rebuked and ignored. The feelings produced by these negative words spoken are also going to be negative feelings, feelings of sadness, discouragement, low self-worth, and despair. The negative feelings produced by negative words are your minds way of letting you know that these negative words are too painful and toxic and that you should not believe them or think them ever again. If you choose to let negative words stay and grow in the garden of your mind you will end up growing and reproducing the sad, discouraging feelings associated with them and eventually, your mind will become a dis-eased place of fear, dread, and torment. You will begin to feel like you need to escape your mind, which is something that you cannot do. You must have more right thoughts growing in the garden of your mind than wrong thoughts. Constantly having an abundance of wrong thoughts in your mind will cause the right thoughts to be ineffective and lead to a double-mind and mental illness.

Test everything against the word and knowledge of Christ

You have the right tools to till the soil of your mind and sort your seeds, now you must dig deep and plant them in the soil of your mind, water them with the word of God and let God's holy spirit be the sunlight that nourishes them and keeps them growing. When you are questioning whether something should be planted in your mind make the word of God your primary fact checker for all questionable thoughts and experiences. In the above example of a wrong thought, we were presented with a thought from an outside source that suggested we are stupid and incompetent. Of course, you know that you are not, but you can check this information using the word of God. If the word of God says something contrary to this, which it does, or proves that this is a lie, then the thought should be ignored and rebuked in the name of Jesus Christ because it has been sent to torment you and oppress you emotionally and mentally.

What does God say about you and your abilities in his word? God calls you loved. God calls you protected. God calls your sins washed by the blood of Jesus. God calls you forgiven. The bible states that you can do all things through Christ who gives you strength (8). God sums it all up when he says to Joshua; Have not I commanded thee? Be strong and of a good courage; be not afraid, neither be thou dismayed; For the Lord, thy God is with thee wherever you go (8). Like Joshua we are called to be strong, courageous, and discerning because maintaining our mental health requires us to be all these things.

There are screenings and check-ups for almost every organ of the body except the mind. For the heart you have EKGs, for the lungs and other organs there are blood tests that measure function. Screenings for the condition of the mind are not performed as often as screenings for other organs of the body. Mental health screenings usually include a list of question about how you have been feeling. Therefore, it is up to us to do mental self-examinations daily. If the thoughts you have been thinking are causing you to feel sad, depressed, anxious, and fearful, this means that they are too heavy for you and are causing you mental pain and anguish. Cast these cares, thoughts, and anxieties to Christ (through prayer). Casting all your cares upon Him (Jesus) for He cares for you (10). You must do this daily. Healthy thinking must begin in the morning as soon as you open your eyes, throughout your day, and at night before you close your eyes to sleep (just like prayer). Developing a healthy thought life is essential if you want to maintain your mental health. Developing a healthy thought life is a life-long process so be patient with yourself and be patient with God. Have faith in the process and you can win the battle of the mind.

CHAPTER 4 PRAYER POINT:

Heavenly Father we thank you for life, salvation, and strength. We seek to serve you with a healthy mind. Create in us a mind and heart that will always point others to you. Help us to develop a mind like yours and a heart that loves and serves you. We know that you came so that we may have life more abundantly and we seek that life by maintain our mental health. We ask for your help and strength in maintaining our mental health. We honor you and we ask these things in the name of your son Jesus. Amen

The Garden of your Mind Looks Amazing!

Part 1

Review

Mental illness can happen to anyone. Regardless of race, title, socioeconomic status, or age. Christians and non-Christians alike. When we learn how to guard our mind, we can prevent mental illness from pulling us into a dark place and ruining our lives. The first step in guarding our minds is developing a deep personal relationship with Christ. A relationship that is full of prayer, faith, love, patience, and hope.

As stated in the introduction, Part 1 of this book was written for younger readers between the ages of 8 and 19. It is designed to teach young people about the importance of maintaining their mental health and how to guard their minds. It is important to learn how to effectively deal with traumatic experiences, verbal abuse, and evil people. When we do not know how to guard our minds, negative experiences and the toxic words of other people will penetrate our minds and cause distress, disease, and illness. You must understand how sacred your mind is! It is your own private and personal space. You are the designer and keeper of your mind and thoughts. You should make sure your mind is always a place that you can retreat to, to feel peace and get still. If your mind is filled with negative thoughts, regrets, bitterness and unforgiveness you will not experience peace in your time of quiet, but you will experience all the emotions and feelings that are produced by being remorseful, angry, bitter, and unforgiving. With a mind filled with negativity, despair, anger, and bitterness it will be harder to experience God's grace and abundance for your life. Remember, it is Gods will that you prosper and be in good health even as your soul prospers (1).

Your mind is your own personal garden, and your thoughts are the seeds. Your mind will cultivate and grow whatever thoughts (seeds) it is given. When it is unguarded, toxic thoughts can get in and grow causing disease and distress. As you work on your relationship with God through the Holy Spirit, you will find the strength and wisdom that you need to help you guard your mind.

To help you keep the garden of your mind fresh, fertile, and beautiful you will need some essential gardening tools. The first and most important tool is salvation, the bible refers to salvation as a helmet. Helmets protect the brain from injury. Prayer will prepare your mind and make it good ground. Prayer is just as important as salvation because it also helps you grow spiritually as well as mentally. The garden tool of discernment will help you to sort the good seeds (or thoughts) from the bad seeds (or thoughts). These tools are closely followed up by reading the word of God and obeying the word of God. Your mind must always be connected to God (the source of life) by meditating on his word day and night. With a mind and heart connected to God you will find protection, wisdom, and understanding. Blessed are those who find wisdom, and those who gain understanding (3).

Next you will have an opportunity to reflect and journal about what you have learned by reading Part 1 of this book. The journal entry is for you to reflect on any thoughts or questions that might have come up regarding your own mental health. Questions like: Do your current thoughts align with the word of God? What can you do to improve your mental health? and what things or people may be causing you mental pain and anguish? Perhaps you would like to jot down some negative thoughts that you tend to think and next to those thoughts you can write down a positive thought or scripture that will defeat the negative thought. For example, if you always think that you are lonely or alone there are several scriptures you can repeat out loud or write down whenever feelings of loneliness arise. Deuteronomy 31:6 says *Be strong and courageous, do not be afraid of any of them, for the Lord your God goes with you, He will never leave you nor forsake you.* (Remember that the feeling of loneliness is produced by constantly thinking thoughts that suggests that you are alone. It might be time to change your thoughts). There are many more scriptures to combat loneliness that are mentioned in the back of this book. In the meantime, please write down whatever is on your mind and heart in the journal pages provided. Like your mind, the journal is your sacred place and what is written in it is confidential; between you and God. Remember there is nothing in your life that is too broken for God to fix. Give him your ashes and he will give you beauty (4).

Part 1

Notes and Reflections

Date: ____________________

Wisdom is the principal thing; therefore, get wisdom: and with all thy getting get understanding (5).

Part 2

*THE DIS-EASED MIND

* As stated in the introduction, part 2 is designed to help you identify and alleviate possible symptoms of a diseased mind (or mental illness). It is not meant to diagnose or treat any illness. Please consult a physician before taking any of the advice listed in this section or go to your local emergency room if you need a diagnosis, treatment and/or counseling. Needing help is okay. Suffering in silence is not okay.

Chapter 1

Identifying and Uprooting Toxic Thoughts

Wherefore seeing that we are compassed about with so great a cloud of witnesses let us lay aside every weight and sin that does so easily beset us and let us run with patience the race that is set before us (1).

When we do not know how to properly deal with pain, disappointment by people, and traumatic experiences we will unknowingly stuff them all into our subconscious and leave them there while we continue to live our lives, form new relationships, and get older. The unfortunate thing about this is that those experiences, thoughts, and memories remain in our subconscious and indirectly dictate our behavior and how we respond to new people and experiences. Packing these negative things away in our subconscious will create a vulnerability within us that will cause us to distance ourselves from other people and make us afraid to form new relationships. Because we are not taught how to bring these thoughts into captivity through the power of the Holy Spirit, we build up walls and defense mechanisms to protect us from further attack in our areas of pain and vulnerability. We choose to cover up and pack the pain deep inside instead of seeking God and godly counsel for deliverance from it. This is because asking for help requires vulnerability. Packing may help in the short-term but long- term packing can have a devastating impact on your mental health. What are some of the hurts, pains, traumas, and disappointments you have not dealt with but have packed up and put away? Could the hidden pain and unforgiveness be the reason you are making poor decisions or not experiencing Gods best for your life?

An example of a person who has packed away trauma and refuses to identify the problem(s) or deal with the pain of the past would be one of a 57-year-old woman with a drug addiction and gambling problem. In this example she loses her paycheck at the local casino (negative behavior). She returns home disappointed and begins to talk to her children about her loss at the casino and during this conversation she says "Well, my father always said I would be a disaster" (a negative thought packed away deep in her subconscious). This is an example of a childhood trauma that has been packed away and never addressed or healed. This unaddressed pain was packed away in the soil of her subconscious mind where it grew. This toxic growth can now be seen in her toxic actions, because it has become the excuse she gives for her negative behavior, even as a middle-aged adult.

The words her father spoke to her when she was young grew in her subconscious, as she got older. They produced feelings (fruits) of sadness, hopelessness, and low self-worth. The words of her father poisoned her mind and kept her from experiencing God's best for her life. You must get the seed of God's word embedded deep in the soil of your mind where it can grow and defeat the lies of the enemy (even if these lies come from a parent or family member). Your mind must be good ground so when the word of God lands on it you will bring forth an abundance of good fruit (2).

Please make no mistake, mental and emotional unpacking is extremely difficult and uncomfortable. Because it is so painful, some individuals will carry pains and traumas from their childhood well into their 60s. Year after year they fight and deal with the same negative thinking patterns and behaviors that they dealt with in their 20's because they never released (or unpacked) these painful experiences and thoughts to God. They just learned how to live with them packed away in their subconscious.

Packing negative experiences and thoughts away in your subconscious gives them a permanent home in your mind. They will sit there and make your mind a place of torment and instability which will lead to a form of mental illness if they are not dealt with as soon as possible. There will come a time when you must ask yourself the question: Could it be time for me to unpack mentally and emotionally?

I had to do this, and unpacking was the most painful part of my mental and emotional healing. Unpacking will lead you to uncover some painful truths about yourself, your family history, and the reason for your bad choices and behaviors. Let me give you an example of the questions that will arise during the unpacking process. I used to think (and get so sad and depressed by this thinking) about how mean, cold, distant, and uncaring my son's father was. I could not stand the sight of him and for years I was so angry and bitter just thinking about him and his horrible parenting skills. But why had I chosen such a person to father a child with? After my mental breakdown I had to start unpacking and getting to the root of the things that were causing me so much pain. There sitting deep in my subconscious were the painful thoughts and experience of my son's father and his actions. I looked at this experience and these feeling again but this time I needed to get rid of them and not just look at them, feel them, and pack them away for a later time. I had to identify why I had chosen this kind of person to share a child with and then uproot and get rid of all the bitterness and negative feelings associated with this experience. So, instead of looking at how horrible of a person he was, I had to dig much deeper to identify what was so broken in me during that time in my life that would lead me to choose this type of emotionally abusive, individual as a person to share a child with. The question, during my emotional unpacking, had become; Stephanie why did you allow this type of individual into your life? The answers shocked me and revealed that I was still carrying all the pain and rejection from my childhood. I began to realize how insecure I was at 23 when I met my son's father (an insecurity that developed in my childhood). I began to realize how desperate I was for love at 23. I realized that at 23 I was still sad and angry that my father abandoned my mother and left her with two little girls to raise on her own. As I looked back at my 23-year-old, self I saw a young woman who had already endured rape, kidnapping, sex trafficking, became a single mother, and was actively abusing drugs all between the ages of 18-23. The real truth was that I was a broken self-destructive young woman when I met my son's father, broken, addicted, double minded and in need of validation from any man to prove that I was desirable. Realizing this truth led to other questions and self- examinations like "Why was I so broken during this time in my life and how do I begin to heal this pain?"

I realized that at 23 years-old my mind was already severely dis-eased and mental illness had begun to set in. At 23 I had stuffed all my previous traumatic experiences deep down in my subconscious (my thinking at that time was that therapy was for weak people who could not control their own mind. Besides no one else in my family was seeing or had ever seen a therapist). However, packing these things away had made me mentally ill and this mental illness led me to make very poor decisions and form unhealthy relationships. I was living while carrying around anger, pain, sadness, guilt, rejection, low self-esteem, no self-worth, no confidence, and no hope for a good future. It would take me 15 years of more pain, poor decisions, and a mental breakdown to face the reality that if I did not start unpacking this stuff, I would not make it past 40 years old.

So, at 37 years old, I started the work. The work that it would take to heal the broken little girl in me so that I could become the woman that God had predestined me to be. I enlisted the help of a licensed therapist and put my complete faith in God's strength and power and not my own (because at that point I knew I had no strength outside of God's supernatural strength). I had to have faith and be confident that he (God) who had begun this good work in me would continue to perform it until the day of Jesus Christ (3). With His help I continue this work even today and it has been an amazing journey. Unpacking is the self-examination that the bible says we must do (4). The word of God speaks about self-examination and making sure our hearts, minds, and intentions are right and pure.

Unpacking unhealthy thinking, emotional pain, and past traumas is like performing mental and emotional surgery on yourself. Prep yourself for this surgery with fervent prayer and fasting. Let God, through the holy spirit always be the physician in charge. This will ensure that the procedure is meaningful, effective and produces good results. Perform this surgery once a day, once a month, once a year, or as needed. Trust that God knows what he is doing even when some trauma and pain seem to be too painful to confront.

The longer you have packed and stuffed trauma into your subconscious the longer it will take to unpack. A 15-year-old teenager may not have as much unpacking to do as a 57-year-old adult. The objective is to start somewhere. It is time to start unpacking negative thoughts, disappointments, fears, and experiences to make room for the love, joy, peace, and the abundant life that God longs to give you.

Having a mind packed with anxiety, negativity, trauma, and sadness will manifest in negative behaviors. These behaviors could be self-doubt, making reckless choices, low self-esteem, over-eating, having multiple sexual partners, eating poorly, lack of physical exercise, drug, or alcohol abuse, being verbally and physically abusive to other people, not wanting to or having the energy to keep up with your personal hygiene, and not wanting to or having the energy to keep your surroundings neat and clean. These are just some examples of the behaviors that are produced by a mind packed with negative toxic thoughts and experiences.

It is important to get still and connect (or re-connect) with God through prayer when you start noticing these behaviors or when someone else brings them to your attention. Once you are aware of your negative behaviors it is important to identify the root of these behaviors. Negative behaviors are symptoms of deep-rooted mental anguish and pain. The solution to these problems can be found in stillness, prayer, and meditation.

Have you unknowingly let toxic thoughts, bad experiences and negative opinions get planted in the garden of your mind and now they are growing into stinky weeds, towering above all the other beautiful plants (thoughts) in the garden of your mind? These negative thoughts will threaten your peace, joy and happiness and prevent new thoughts of hope, courage, and peace from taking root and growing.

This happened to me. When I was younger it seemed as though one experience after another had been strategically designed to show me how unimportant, stupid, and ugly I was. Because I had not been taught how important my mind was or how to guard my mind, over time, these thoughts and experiences became planted in the garden of my mind and began to grow. They caused me to develop constant negative thinking patterns that eventually became my own personal beliefs about myself. So, in my young mind I saw myself as a sad, helpless, self-defeated young woman full of anxiety and hopelessness. These feelings set me up to make so many careless and reckless decisions in my young-adult life. I let these experiences, thoughts, and beliefs along with the negative opinions of other people become my truth (because I had not yet accepted and embraced God's truth about who I was in him). I continually allowed strangers, toxic friends, and family members to plant garbage and toxic seeds in the garden of my mind and eventually my mind became a garbage dumb instead of a peaceful garden. I did not know how to change this or that I even had the power to change my own mind. (This is mainly because I was not taught how to guard my mind and heart). Through this book, my hope is that if you have found yourself tangled up in the lies of the enemy or toxic people, that you will learn how to properly identify and uproot these thoughts and renew your mind, getting your mind ready for the planting of good thoughts, ideas. and beliefs. The power is within you to renew and change your mind.

Throughout my entire childhood and most of my young adulthood, I soaked up my negative traumatic experiences and other people's negative opinions of me like a dry sponge. With these things in my mind along with my own negative self-image, and the negative images of African Americans in the news and media, my mind was severely dis-eased and distressed by the age of 18. What added to this distress was having to watch my uncles who I loved dearly, lose their battle with drug addiction, and die prematurely. At 18 years old I started showing signs of mental di-ease. I knew at 18 that something was not right within my mind and that I might need help but (in the African American community) asking for help was a sign of weakness and would be embarrassing (so I continued to live the best I could with a diseased mind). 7 years and 2 kids later I was diagnosed with Bi-Polar disorder, post-partum depression and Psychosis. But I was not ready to admit that I was mentally sick because admitting that I was mentally sick at 23 years old was (and often still is) frowned upon in many African American families. Unfortunately, my kids had to be temporarily removed from my custody by CPS who made me seek proper mental health treatment if I ever wanted to get them back.

Yes! That is how bad it had gotten. Other people had started to notice my mental distress (through my behaviors), but I was still too embarrassed to ask for help until I was forced to. Looking back, I realized that it was divine intervention. I really needed that help and God did what he needed to do to get me the help I desperately needed. Thankfully, my children were very young at the time, 8 months old and 4 years old. So, I accepted the help and began the work of processing all the pain and trauma that I had stuffed into my subconscious and refused to deal with. I was 25 years-old at the time and a single mom, homeless with an infant and toddler. Three months after my diagnosis, I was prescribed medication that helped me focus and get my children back. I did this for the next 13 years. I accomplished a lot during those years. I had many successes as well as failures during this time. I learned a lot about myself and about how to properly address the pain and traumas of my past. I learned that growth and healing only stop when life ends. It is a beautiful process if we allow God to do the healing and pruning that is necessary.

Ten years later and after my mental breakdown, I found out that there were some generational curses in my family that I had unknowingly been operating under as a young adult. I needed to know how denounce these generational curses. Although I was doing the work, taking medication, and engaging in therapy these things did not address the spiritual turmoil, warfare, and damage I was suffering. I was getting the help, but I was still unstable, indecisive, and double-minded. I believe that this spiritual warfare is what led to my mental breakdown at 35 years-old even though I had started taking medication and engaging in counseling, and therapy at 25 years-old. (One day during the early stages of my mental healing process, while in prayer, I was shown through the Holy Spirit, how to break and denounce the generational curses that had been troubling me for a long time). I was double-minded and unstable until I began to pray and seek God for wisdom, strength, and courage. The bible states that a double minded person is unstable in everything they do (5).

I want to encourage you to please seek help if you feel that you are having trouble thinking the right thoughts or making the right choices. Do not let mental disease go unchecked. Do not try to fix your mental anguish on your own by using drugs, alcohol, sex, or over-eating. Especially if you have experienced deep pain, trauma, loss, or grief. If you do not seek professional help for mental pain and disease, they will grow into an illness that will cause you to seek relief in other forms that could create addictions and physical illness. If you do begin to overeat, overwork, abuse alcohol or drugs, get into unhealthy relationships, or even consider self-harm or suicide, please forgive yourself and ask God to give you the strength to seek the wisdom and counsel of spiritual and psychological professionals. You are never alone. There is always hope.

CHAPTER 1 PRAYER POINT:

God, I come before your throne confessing and asking forgiveness for my sins, the sins of my fathers and all sins that we have committed against those made in your image. I ask you to deliver me from all double-mindedness, doubt, and unbelief. Show me the thoughts, beliefs, people, and experience that are keeping me oppressed and broken. Show me how to place my brokenness at your feet and to believe you for my mental, spiritual, and emotional healing. I ask you and believe you for these things in Jesus' name. Amen

Chapter 2

What Matters Most?

> And Jesus answered and said unto her, Martha, Martha, thou are careful and troubled about many things: But one thing is needful: and Mary has chosen that part, which shall not be taken away from her. (1)

Have you considered that perhaps you are carrying around burdens and cares that belong to God? Are you fighting battles that you should be giving to God in prayer and letting Him fight them? Perhaps you have been helping people who are not helpless but lazy and full of excuses. Are you constantly thinking about things (from your past and future) that cause you pain, sadness, and anxiety? Have you completely forgiven yourself? Have you completely forgiven those who have offended and wounded you? Are you holding on to bad thoughts and experiences? Are you keeping busy to avoid dealing with your mental and spiritual pain? (Please feel free to answer these questions separately in the journal pages provided at the end of this section). It is important to which things matter and which things do not.

There are certain things that you should think on and meditate on and there are certain things that you should never give a second thought. We must use the spirit of discernment to weed out the thoughts that will cause us to feel sad, defeated, depressed, suicidal, fearful, always busy, anxious, and bitter. There is nothing worse than wasted time. Wasting time doing the wrong things, thinking the wrong thoughts, and keeping company with miserable people. A spirit of discernment will help you properly identify toxic thoughts, people, relationships, and situations. If you have not been using your discernment, start right now. Ask the Father (through the Holy Spirit) to show you exactly what thoughts and toxic people may need to exit your mind, heart, and life. This will help you as you start the process of renewing your mind and save you years of wasted time building toxic, unproductive relationships that are going to leave you broken and empty. Use the tool of discernment every day in every situation. Prayer activates the spirit of discernment. Along with using the spirit of discernment, practice putting away (denouncing) all sin, bitterness, malice, jealousy, strife, and envy that may be present in your life. Cut ties with toxic people. Sever toxic communications and stay away from friends and family who willingly and openly practice sin. You will be giving your mind and heart a break by doing this. You will also avoid sending your mind into a state of total break-down.

There is only so much abuse and pain our minds and bodies can tolerate. Thankfully, they are set up to warn us (through pain signals such as sadness) long before a break down occurs that they are suffering and that you are subjecting them to too many painful, toxic thoughts and substances. This is the beauty of the human body, spirit, and mind. God has designed our entire being to signal us when we encounter distress or when we have ingested anything poisonous by producing pain signals.

Listen to your body. If you have been feeling extremely depressed, oppressed, anxious, sad, or overwhelmed – This simply means that the thoughts, experiences, or beliefs that you are carrying in your mind are too heavy or too toxic thus producing these negative feelings (or pain signals). When you eat something that is bad or toxic your body will respond with pain. You will experience stomach cramps, nausea, headaches, vomiting and other unpleasant symptoms. So, it is with your mind, it responds the same way as your body does when a harmful food or substance is taken in. However, the pain that the mind produces is different than the pain responses of the body. When a toxic thought, experience, or word enters the mind, the pain signals that the mind produces is in the form of negative feelings and emotions. You will know if a thought or experience is toxic if it immediately produces feelings of sadness, anxiety, fear, oppression, depression, anger, or low self-worth; When you do feel these negative feelings, your mind is telling you that a particular thought or experience is not good and is producing pain. For example, when someone calls you dumb, stupid or useless you immediately feel sad and hopeless. Whether or not these words are true your mind has heard them and is now trying to process them. Because the words are toxic and poisonous the mind will immediately produce feelings of anger and sadness (these feelings are pain signals). Instead of holding on to the negative words and the anger and sadness they have produced, look at the negative feelings as your minds way of identifying the words as toxic and painful. To combat these toxic words, recall and recite the scripture that says God had not given us the spirit of fear but of power, love, and a sound mind. Understand that toxic words are always spoken by someone with a toxic, diseased mind themselves. Do not try to understand why people say the things that they say, that is not your job. Your job is to protect and guard your mind and heart from receiving and believing the toxic words of others. Forgive the person who has spoken negative toxic words about you or over you and pray for their mental and emotional healing. Remember that "a good man out of the good treasure of his heart bringeth forth that which is good; and an evil man out of the evil treasure of his heart brings forth that which is evil. For of the abundance of his heart his mouth speaks" (2). The saying that "hurting people, hurt other people" is true.

Are you the individual (like myself) who started receiving, believing, and carrying negative toxic thoughts around and letting them contaminate the garden of your mind? Now it is as if they have become over-grown weeds and you have no peace or clarity. Do you feel like you do not know who you are because the negative words of others have destroyed your self-image, your joy, peace, and purpose? Part 2 of this book is for you. I want to help you recalibrate your mind, dig up those over-grown weeds, re-till the soil of your mind and get it ready to receive the good news of Jesus Christ, news of love, joy, peace, and righteousness.

As dark as it may look, as tormented as your mind may be right now, there is hope! But you must get still, quite yourself, and get a clear understanding of what is at the root of the mental anguish and dis-ease you have been feeling. Once you have done the work of identifying them, you can begin to dig them up and toss them out.

While you are in your moments of stillness, ask yourself questions like: are you carrying things that are too heavy for you? Are you carrying your traumas in your mind and on your back like a 1000-pound sack? Are you carrying unforgiveness? Are you fighting battles that do not belong to you but belong to God? Are you operating under a generational curse brought on by the sins of your parents and grandparents? What could have led you to make all the bad choices that you have made?

I will be honest about this part of the mind renewal process: It may be very painful. Because it is going to require that you stare the trauma, bad choices, and your past square in the eye. The mental healing process is never easy, which is why so many people do not do it. They stay stuck in this mental anguish rather than examine the reason for their negative thoughts and self-destructive behaviors because pointing the finger at other people is easier than examining and changing ourselves and our behaviors.

However, remaining stuck in a state of mental illness is more painful than the healing process and will eventually lead to a mental, physical, or emotional death. Begin the work of mental healing as soon as you are aware of the mental dis-ease. Do not wait until your mind becomes too ill to function and stops doing so. You will require hospitalization if it gets to this point. Remember, you must take your mind with you everywhere you go. Begin treating your mind and mental health as you would your most prized possession because that is exactly what they are.

Beloved, please take as long as you need to retrain and renew your mind. I took 20 years. You may not need that long, or you may need more time. This process is not a race. It is a process that requires time. Be patient with yourself during this process. Especially at the beginning. Do not put a time limit on your mental healing and well-being. Everyone's process looks different.

Understand that this process is a life-long journey and although it took me 20 years to renew my mind, I have just begun the process of living my life through the lens of my renewed mind. I do not want it to take you 20 years. I am writing this section of my book to help you through the process so you will only need 2 years to see the fruits of a healthy, renewed mind instead of 20. Renewing your mind is a daily process. As you begin this process it is important to live in the present. Do not live in the past because you will be operating in the spirit of regret and depression and not live in the future because you will be operating in the spirit of anxiety and fear. But begin by being thankful and mindful for the present moment and the fact that you have started the journey. This will allow you to focus and live in a spirit of gratitude which opens you up to experience supernatural healing, miracles, and the spirit of peace.

As you begin to renew your mind every day will look and feel different. You will find (as I did) that some days you will have a great deal of insight and revelation, and other days you will not have the mental strength to do much digging up and tossing out of old thinking patterns and thoughts. This is okay. Know that the days that seem unproductive are a part of the process and they are developing and building your patience. You have an infinite amount of time to do the work. There is no due date or deadline. On the days that you feel powerless, pray, and give yourself some grace to simply begin the work again when you have the strength to do so.

Renewing your mind is like spring cleaning. Spring cleaning usually happens as the winter season is ending, the sun begins to shine brighter and longer, and the warmer weather can be seen and felt. Spring cleaning is done with the anticipation of a new season and to make room for all the wonderful things that a new season brings. During spring cleaning, people usually open the windows of the house that have been shut all winter to keep out the cold; inviting the warm spring air into the home and releasing the old, stale air accumulated in the home during the winter months. Spring cleaning also includes the sweeping out of anything old accumulated during the winter and making room for the new growth and new life that comes along with every Spring. Flowers are planted and gardens are prepared to receive new seeds that will yield an abundant fall harvest. It is a beautiful time.

Although the mental renewal process can be very painful, it is important to look at the bigger picture. Look at it as mental spring cleaning, that is, making room for new things (thoughts and ideas) to grow and doing away with the old that no longer serves a purpose. A time to sweep out the old thoughts, relationships, and habits that have been blocking our spiritual, physical, and emotional growth and causing so much mental anguish. You can even start renewing your mind after one painful thing (relationship, time, or season) ends and before any new thing begins. You may even wish to begin the process of renewing your mind during the changing of seasons. Whenever you decide to begin, be sure to begin with prayer, meditation, a mustard seed of faith, a grateful heart, and a great deal of expectation and anticipation for something new and wonderful to take place. Keep a journal close by during this time to record your thoughts and feelings and any revelations you receive through the Holy Spirit.

Finding time dedicated to prayer, meditation and stillness is just as important as finding time for breakfast, lunch, and dinner. After all, time spent in prayer is what will help restore, feed, nourish your mind and spirit. Just as you find the time to feed your body you must find the time to feed your mind, spirit, and soul. The things that you choose to meditate on (or continually think about) also serves as food and fuel for your mind and spirit. Find the time for prayer, meditation, and reflection. Feed your mind the word of God along with other sources of spiritual wisdom and knowledge.

CHAPTER 2 PRAYER POINT:

Father God, I thank you for all that you have done. I thank you for new beginnings, new mercies, and new revelations. I humbly ask you to give me the strength to begin the process of renewing my mind. I confess that the way that I have been thinking and living is not bringing glory to myself, others, or you. I humble myself and I turn from my negative and sinful ways of thinking and living. I ask you for the patience, faith, wisdom, strength, and confidence I need to begin the process of renewing my mind. I believe that you will lead me and guide me into the truth of who you are and who I am in you. In Jesus name I pray this prayer. Amen

Chapter 3

Boundaries and Expectations

> Beloved, believe not every spirit, but try the spirits whether they are of God: because many false prophets have gone out into the world (1).

As you are renewing your mind and uprooting toxic thoughts and behaviors this will also be a good time to make sure your personal boundaries and expectations are clear and realistic. According to the Oxford Languages Dictionary (2020), a boundary is a line that marks the limits of an area. Where are the boundaries in your spiritual and mental life? Are people allowed to get too close to you with their evil deeds and words? Where do you draw your boundary lines? When a person abuses you do you continue to accept the abuse? When someone continually mistreats and offends you, do you still allow them to have access to you?

Boundaries are extremely important because they create a limit as to what people can say and do to you. Boundaries are not only good for your relationships with other people but also with yourself. Setting healthy boundaries and expectation for yourself is also necessary. Self-imposed boundaries can be things like only eating healthy foods and committing to not putting toxic foods and substances in your body. Another healthy boundary or expectation can be that you do not allow people to use profanity while having a conversation with you (this is one I have recently adopted). If someone want to have a conversation with me, I make it clear that I do not use foul language and that I will not let them use it while speaking to me. I let them know this, and if they do not mind, then the conversation can continue, but if they want to continue to use profanity then our conversation stops immediately.

There must be certain things that you will never allow from yourself or others. Allowing anything to go one in your life or allowing people to do and say anything they want to you will overtime break you down mentally. You may want to write these boundaries down in your journal or prayer book. As you begin to renew your mind, you will form new boundaries because as you do the work of unpacking and healing you will find that the reason for some of your mental pain was because you chose to accept, tolerate, and entertain negative situations and people for way too long. Setting healthy boundaries and expectations will help you maintain your spiritual peace and mental health. Start stetting healthy boundaries and realistic expectations today!

Double Mindedness

Having a double mind means that you are not consistent in your thoughts and beliefs. This kind of inconsistency will spill over into your actions, daily decisions, and even the words you speak. It will not only cause your mind to be a place of torment and confusion but your life as well. I operated in a state of double mindedness for most of my young adult life. Because of my double mindedness coupled with constant demonic attacks on my life (attacks of sexual abuse at 14, drug abuse at 17, and being kidnapped and sex trafficked at 19), I found myself in full mental breakdown that required hospitalization, medication, and intense therapy at the age of 35.

An example of double mindedness is saying that you are a Christian while living with a mind and heart full of doubt, anger, sin, and unbelief. Your thoughts must match your actions. You must have consistent faith and believe that you will one day be able to overcome the traumas of your past, forgive yourself and all those who have wrong you, and break generational curses. Remember that it is not going to happen overnight but being consistent and steadfast in your walk with Christ will eventually ensure your victory in every other area of life. Be patient and walk by faith.

Faith is being sure of the things we cannot yet see (3). When I was 20 years old, I was so depressed, discouraged, and sad that I could not see myself emotionally healed, happy and whole at 40. However, I refused to stop believing God's best for my life even during the darkest times of my life. That was my faith, to believe that what I could not yet see at 20 years old (healing, happiness, peace, and wholeness) would one day be possible. Today, (and because of my faith over those 20 years) I live the happy, whole, peaceful life I imagined over 20 years ago. I wake up to a healed, happy whole mind and life because of and by my faith. The Bible is full of so many examples of the things that were (and still can be) done by faith (4).

To bring your mind and heart back into singleness or wholeness (5) you must live and think in a singular way. Meaning, that you must live one way, be dedicated to one thing, one mindset, and one God. Peace and prosperity come from keeping your mind and heart fixed on, and full of the truth of God. Singleness of mind means that you do not have many conflicting thoughts, behaviors, or beliefs. It is the opposite of being double-minded. Other examples of a single mind are, meditating on the word of God and then living a life that reflects the word of God, and having faith and then doing the works that your faith requires you to do (6). Another example of single-mindedness is when we say that we trust God, we trust him in all things not just the little things but the big things too. We must trust God to heal us from the pain and trauma of our past just as we trust him to provide for us and our families every day.

When my mind became severely dis-eased at the age of 24, I filled my life with more illicit sex, drugs and continued in my double mindedness. I decided to numb the mental pain, instead of getting still, getting quiet and turning to my creator. The symptoms of my diseased mind included double minded thinking, prolonged feeling of sadness and crying, excessive spending and eating, indulging in toxic self-defeating thoughts and habits. I also had thoughts of suicide and low self-worth which led me to develop unhealthy relationships with toxic individuals. Adding to my mental dis-ease were the generational curses I was unknowingly operating under. The generational curses were showing up in my life as oppression, addiction, poverty, hopelessness, and continual disobedience.

You can identify a generational curse when you see that it has happened to your mother and grandmother and then you and those closely related to you by blood. Being unable to thrive, grow, and always thinking negative thoughts, extreme poverty and having many children outside of the covenant of marriage are all signs of generational curses; especially if these signs move from one generation to the next. Rape, trauma, incest, hopelessness, the inability to think clearly and make proper decisions are also signs of generational curses. Be patient and do not be afraid. These curses take time, patience, obedience, and the power of Gods spirit to fall off your life and the lives of future generations. Breaking generational curses cannot be done with medication, it takes fervent and constant prayer coupled with fasting and obedience to God. It is a spiritual war, and you must use spiritual weapons to defeat and pull down these strong-holds (7).

CHAPTER 3 PRAYER POINT:

Father God, I thank you for your strength and your holy spirit that enables me to do all things well. I ask that you allow your holy spirit to give me the necessary courage to set boundaries when things and people come to destroy my joy and peace. Grant me the spirit of discernment to set proper boundaries and expectations. Teach me how to walk in single mindedness. In Jesus' name I ask and pray. Amen

Chapter 4

Stillness and Quiet

> He leads me beside the still waters, He restores my soul (1).

Now that you have learned how to identify the toxic thoughts, behaviors, people, experiences, childhood traumas, lies and possible generational curses that have been tormenting your mind and life, it is time for you to get still. When your mind experiences discomfort or becomes diseased it is simply telling you that there are some things (thoughts, memories, experiences, or beliefs) inside of it that are causing pain and making it very sick. The negative emotions that you feel when you think about or relive a traumatic experience is your minds way of asking you to STOP thinking those things or stop reliving those experiences immediately. Our bodies work the same way. When you drink milk that is bad you will get a signal from your stomach in the form of pain or vomiting. This pain is also telling you that the milk is bad and please do not drink it again. Vomiting is the body way of rejecting the bad milk. Sadness, depression, anxiety, and low self-worth are all signals and symptoms of bad thoughts and experiences overwhelming the mind. Signals and symptoms carry important messages. Do not ignore them. They are telling you that your thoughts and actions are producing this sadness, depression, and anxiety. You should stop thinking these thoughts immediately because they are toxic and harmful to your mental health. Sadness is always produced by meditating on sad memories or thoughts.

When you feel sadness, fear, anxiety or depression, your mind is warning you that your thoughts are harmful and that you need to renew your way of thinking. When this happens, it is time to for you to get Still! Do not continue to feed your mind these negative experiences or thoughts and do not continue to keep company with negative speaking people.

The phrase "*be still*" is first seen in the Bible spoken by Jesus as he was commanding a raging storm to cease (2). When there is a raging storm of negative thoughts, anger, sadness, and self-doubt in your mind, and you feel like you will drown mentally; take a deep breath and speak these words to yourself; "*Be still, my soul.*" It is impossible to be at peace mentally and spiritually and live a prosperous life when the thoughts in your mind are always raging. A raging mind will lead to a chaotic life and produce bad fruit (or negative behaviors). Behaviors that are hurtful to us and to others. Behaviors that include lying, cheating, stealing, plotting the downfall of others, betraying others, sexual immorality, physically hurting and manipulating others, jealousy, envy, and hatred of others and self all come from a sick, raging, dis-eased mind. You cannot be an effective

Christian with a mind that is dis-eased and always raging. The scripture is worth repeating, when Jesus says "a good man out of the good treasures of his heart brings forth that which is good: and an evil man out of the evil treasures of his heart brings forth that which is evil, for of the abundance of the heart the mouth speaks (3)"

It is so important to do a daily self-examination of the contents of your mind and heart. Make sure they line up with the word of God. Everything that you say and do reflects the things that are in your heart and mind and will reveal whether those things are good or evil. I encourage you to examine the contents of your mind and heart every day and getting still will help you do that.

Getting still will require that you set aside time for stillness and reflection each day. Implementing a simple breathing meditation technique can help you get the most out of your time of stillness. This stillness will create a peaceful space in which you can examine your thoughts, renew your mind, hear from God, and begin to deal with the emotional traumas of your past (you do not have to do this until you feel emotionally and mentally strong enough). The breathing meditation only requires 5 minutes of your day and will help you to quiet your mind. You can take more time if needed, but to start you only need to set aside 5 minutes per day. Remember to go at your own pace, meaning that you might be able to start this meditation, but you may not be ready to start mentally unpacking during or immediately after your 5-minute meditation. You may need to begin by using this time to just quiet your mind and gather the strength to begin mentally unpacking in six months or a year from the time you begin this practice. I suggest that you pray before each 5- minute mediation session. Pray and let your specific requests be made known to God. Especially if you would like to start using the mediation time to seek answers to the hard questions like "why am I making poor decisions?' or Why do I continue to let toxic people occupy my space?" Ask God for the strength to handle the answers to the difficult questions. The answers will not come right away but they will come when you are ready to humbly receive and deal with them. I can tell you this was the hardest part of my mental healing journey. I did not fully embrace this part of the healing process until 2 years after my mental breakdown because the answers I received to my difficult questions were extremely painful.

However, I knew that to get to a better place mentally, spiritually, and emotionally, I would have to do the hardest work of my life. But, after a while, this hard work allowed me to find the source and roots of some of my deepest emotional pains. Pain that had led me to believe lies about myself and to make self-destructive decisions. Eventually, God gave me the strength to accept my past mistakes, (the ones that I could not change) change the things that I could change, and the things that I did not understand or could not change I surrendered to him.

You will need to be emotionally prepared to deal with the painful answers associated with unpacking past traumas and disappointments. Some of the roots of our mental anguish as adults are rooted deep in childhood and young adulthood. You will have to dig deep to get to the source(s). One example of something very difficult that may come up during this time of stillness, reflection, and revelation is the fact that some of the closest people to you (parents, siblings, childhood friends, spouse, church) are toxic individuals who are secretly jealous of you and want to see you fail. You might also discover that to get the most out of your time of mental healing and renewal, you need to relocate to another state or city (completely removing yourself from the toxic individuals and environments). I used this example because this is what happened to me during the early stages of my mental healing (a healing that continues to this day).

Take as much time as you need to become comfortable in your time of stillness and meditation. But be sure to fit it into each day. It is a time in which all distractions cease, and you are alone with God, your mind, and your thoughts. It will also give your mind rest and allow it to be free from negative thoughts or over-thinking. It is a time in which you are to just BE; be still, be present, be mindful, and be hopeful.

In a time of stillness and meditation, some people like to light candles and play soft soothing music. Whatever you choose to do during this time is fine. This time of stillness and reflection can be the same or different every day. It can be done sitting on a bench at your favorite local park, a long drive by yourself, or sitting on the edge of your bed at 4 am. Your time of stillness must always be free of distractions. During this time take a moment to reflect on the beauty around you or just sit and feel every breath you are taking.

Life is not always about rushing, working, or keeping busy. Rest, reflection, and stillness are so important that God made them a commandment. God commanded Israel to not only remember the sabbath day but to set it aside as a day of rest and reflection. A day in which they did absolutely no work (4). It happens to be my favorite commandment! I look forward to my Sabbath day. Sometimes it is spent with my children and other times we get together for worship with other believers. It is a day to rest and reflect on the goodness and faithfulness of God. We all need at least 24 hours of stillness, silence, rest, and reflection per week. Scripture commands that we take the entire 24 hours during the Sabbath. But if you cannot do this right away, start by taking small steps; try taking 30 minutes after waking up and 30 minutes before you go to sleep to just breathe deeply, pray, be still, and enter God's presence with thanksgiving for all the things you have. Remember everything takes time to master. Give yourself a little grace and patience as you carve out time for stillness and re-train your mind to think good healthy thoughts.

CHAPTER 4 PRAYER POINT:

Heavenly Father I thank you for your grace, mercy, and truth. Father as I renew my mind create in me a burning desire for your presence, your word, and your holy spirit. I realize that I cannot be successful in my life's journey without these things. Help me to be still and focus on your goodness and your love for me. I love you and I thank you for all things. In Jesus Name I pray. Amen

Part 2

Review

The prefix "dis" means to be apart from or disconnected from something (Oxford Dictionary, 2021). When something, such as the mind becomes dis-eased it means that the mind is not in its original eased or peaceful state and has now become (dis)eased. Part 2 of this book looks at the different ways the mind can get to this dysfunctional or dis-eased state. You will usually begin to see the symptoms of a diseased mind in young adulthood. When negative thoughts and childhood traumas go unresolved and are suppressed in our subconscious they will resurface through our behaviors. It is okay to ask for help when things happen that hurt us deeply. It is not okay to suffer in silence.

Speak to someone and tell them you are having a hard time processing the pain, disappointments, and trauma you have experienced. If you stuff the pain deep down inside it does NOT go away. It will manifest in over-eating, over-sexing, drug, and alcohol abuse, along with the abuse of yourself and mistreatment of other people. Can you see how those things could prevent you from being an effective witness for Christ? It will be very hard to share Christ if you are abusing and mistreating yourself and others. The Bible tells us to "lay aside every weight and sin that so easily besets (or troubles) us (2).

Seeking wise counsel regarding sensitive issues of the mind and heart is the second step in the mental healing process - The first step is recognizing and accepting the fact that you need help processing what has happened to you or a loved one – those who are wise and Godly are going to be able to help you both emotionally and spiritually. Christian counseling or (therapy) is becoming very popular. I recommend this type of counseling especially for practicing Christians who have had traumatic experiences and need help processing these experiences from a biblical point of view.

Most of us never learn how to deal with sadness, loss, grief, disappointments, and childhood traumas. So instead of dealing with these issues or asking for help in dealing with these issues we stuff them down and keep going. But when we do not properly deal with trauma and negative experiences, they will cause our minds to become distressed and cause us to say things and act in ways that hurt us and other people. I have included a list of resources in the back of this book that you can use if you are experiencing a mental health crisis. Do not wait too long to seek professional help. Until you get still and get the help you need you will unintentionally say and do things to hurt yourself and those around you. When our minds are hurting and in distress from carrying around painful traumatic experiences, we will make bad decisions, hurt other people, and say hurtful things. Because hurting people often hurt other people it is important to forgive as soon as possible when we are hurt or offended by others and not carry the hurt and pain around with us.

The following pages are included for you to write down anything that comes to mind. Use these pages as your own prayer and thought journal. You may need to reflect on the thoughts you need to change. What relationships need to be strengthened? Which relationships need to end? Write down the names of those you still need to forgive. Perhaps you can write about something that is causing you fear.

Like your mind the journal is your sacred place to be open and honest with yourself and with God. Go to God in truth and lay everything down at his feet. If you are struggling with sin. Let him know. If you are struggling with addiction. Let him know. (He knows anyway and wants to help you). Use the journal to keep track of the things you wish to see change in your life. Be patient and remember life is a journey, do not make it about a destination. You can have joy and peace through Christ during this process.

Part 2

Notes & Reflection

Date: ____________________

Part 3

*MENTAL ILLNESS

* Part three of this book is designed to help those who are currently in full mental break down, have experienced a mental break down or know someone who is in the middle of a mental crisis. It is not meant to treat or diagnose any mental illness. Please consult a health professional or go to your local emergency room if you need a diagnosis, are not feeling safe, or need to talk to someone. This is not the end. It is a beautiful new beginning.

Chapter 1

The Darkest Hour

> And he said unto me, my strength is sufficient for you: for my power is made perfect in weakness. Therefore, I will boast all the more gladly about my weaknesses, so that Christ's power may rest upon me. (1)

A mental illness is a medical condition that disrupt a person's thinking, mood, daily functioning, and ability to relate to others (2). When you are in the grip of a mental illness you must seek medical attention right away. The earlier parts of this book talked about how to prevent a mental crisis. However, you may have started reading this book during your own mental health crisis. If this is the case, then I would suggest that you seek professional help before your mental situation causes you to make any irreversible self-destructive decisions.

When I was at this point it was essentially the darkest hour of my life. I was raising two kids, had little support and felt the world would be better off without me. I was 34 and I had given life and everyone in my life all I could give. I had cared for and loved everyone but myself, and unknowingly neglected my own mental health and safety to do so. There I was in the darkest hour of my life, working, going to church every Sunday, raising kids, and in the middle of a mental crisis. I needed help. *"But I was always the strong one. The one caring for everyone else. I could bounce back from anything"* I thought to myself. But not this time...and I knew it. I knew I needed to seek help, or I was not only going to continue to die mentally but I would eventually succumb to a physical death and my children did not deserve that. So, I laid down my prideful spirit and checked myself into a mental hospital. What I did not realize at that moment was that it was the beginning of a beautiful, brave, humbled, renewed version of life.

Asking for Help

In the African American culture, admitting to a mental illness is like saying "*I am crazy, and I don't know why.*" It is admitting you are weak and cannot handle or control your own mind. The unspoken cure is "just pray and everything will be fine". The thing with prayer is that it is to be used to prevent a mental health crisis not while you are in the middle of one. Prayer is like medicine that is taken as needed to keep you in perfect peace. Meaning that, if you constantly fill your mind and life with lies, sin, and disobedience ultimately you will experience a mental health crisis.

Once you are in a mental crisis it is going to take more than prayer to start and be successful in renewing your mind. This is when you need to seek professional help from psychologists and psychiatrists in your local area. Asking for help is not easy. We do not know what to say or we wonder what our friends and family will think about us. The truth is this: it is your life, and you need to get better. Worrying about the opinion of friends and family (who's negative, nasty words have most likely contributed to your mental health crisis) is not going to help you get better. My biggest problem was thinking "*What will people think?*" This thought kept me from seeking the help that I knew that I needed at 19 and letting my mental health deteriorate to a point where hospitalization was no longer optional but necessary. Needing help is okay! You are not weak, and you are not crazy. What has happened is that you have overwhelmed your mental capacity and you just kept going. Instead of dealing with past traumas you kept stuffing them down and packing them away. You continued to let toxic people speak lies and negativity into your mind, heart, and life. You let these lies become your truth and now your mind has said "enough!" It is saying "I can no longer function under these negative conditions!" A mental crisis is your brains way of screaming for help, for peace, for comfort, and rest. Asking for help is a sign of strength and wisdom. You are acknowledging that something is wrong and that you want to change for the better. Deciding to ask for help is the beginning of your mental healing journey. Take it from me, it is the best decision you will ever make. Beloved, it is time to truly lay those heavy, toxic thoughts, burdens, and behaviors down. They are too heavy for you! Lay them down at the feet of Jesus and just rest.

Trust The Process

I will not mislead to you or lie to you. If you wish to renew your mind and come back strong from mental crisis or illness, it is going to be hard work. It will not be easy, but it will be worth it. Whenever it seems too tough to keep going remember that You can do all things through Christ who strengthens you (3). Your process is not going to look like everyone else's. Do not compare your healing process to anyone or anything else. This is your journey take as long as you need and do what is required to make this journey as successful as possible for you. After you are evaluated by a professional you may or may not need to take medication(s) to ease your mental anguish. These medicines will help you while you do the work required to heal past traumas. Think of them as the anesthesia required to do mental surgery, like the anesthesia given to numb the pain of birth. Do not frown upon taking psychiatric medications if it is necessary.

In the African American community, taking psychiatric medication is often discouraged and mocked. Others may view you as weak, crazy, or fragile. Those who make you feel this way must be removed from your life immediately (if possible) or they will hinder your progress. Remember, this is your journey, not theirs, and you must do what is best for you to function properly and continue the process of healing. Sometimes that means taking a prescribed medication and speaking with a licensed therapist. Whatever your healing process requires take joy in the fact that it has finally begun. [Always] Be confident of this very thing, that He who has begun (this) good work in you is faithful to complete it until the day of Jesus Christ (4).

Is this your fight?

Now that you have started the mental healing process you are going to need all your strength and energy to sort through and pluck out the negative people, thoughts, pain, and experiences that no longer serve you. You will need to know what changes need to be made to continue to heal and renew your mind. Remember that you will be using the spirit of discernment to get rid of the toxic behaviors, negative people, and destructive relationships.

During this time, you will still be living your daily life, making basic decisions, interacting with your children, certain family members, strangers, and friends. Grocery shopping, doctor's appointments, High School graduations and life in general will continue to happen while you are renewing your mind and healing the pain of your past. Life and time do not stop when we need a rest to renew and strengthen ourselves. Knowing how to guard your already fragile state of mind from outside attacks while you are in the mind renewal process is extremely important. (Yes, attacks and negative experiences will still happen during this time!). It is more important than ever to know how to pick and choose your battles wisely. This is the time that you must learn to stop giving your (limited) mental energy to petty arguments, insecure people and small things sent to disturb your peace. The Holy spirit along with the spirit of discernment will help you do this. Most of life's battles belong to God and some battles are for you to stand and fight through prayer, faith and fasting. Usually, the battles that God gives us to fight, are to strengthen us in an area we are weak. When we are done with the battles given to us by God, we will always come out stronger, more confident, and victorious. Just remember that some things and people require your attention and some things and people absolutely do not! When challenges and negativity are presented to you, make sure to ask yourself (and God through prayer) *"Is this my fight or God's?"* Knowing this will save you from wasting your time, strength and energy on battles that belong to the Lord. Start learning how to cast all your cares (worries and anxieties) upon the Lord, because He (the Lord) cares (deeply) for you (5).

CHAPTER 1 PRAYER POINT:

Father God, we thank you for allowing us to see that apart from you we are weak and that we cannot live this life abundantly without your Holy Spirit, peace, protection, and provision. Help us to lay aside every weight and sin that so easily besets us and run this race with peace, patience, joy, and thanksgiving. We cast all our cares to you. As your sheep we look to you to feed us, clothe us, protect us, and lead us beside calm still waters. Walk this journey with us Father and renew a right heart, mind, and spirit within us daily. In Jesus name we ask and receive. Amen

Chapter 2

Renewing your Mind

Let this mind be in you that was also in Christ Jesus (1)

The image on the front cover and other images throughout this book were picked out for a specific reason. These images are there to give you thoughts and feelings of peace, joy, and safety. Your eyes and ears are the channels to your mind because most of our thoughts and experiences enter our minds through these two gates. Most of the mental torment and past trauma we have suffered are from things we have heard and/or seen. It is so important to make sure that you are allowing yourself to see and hear good things because these things become memories and cannot be unheard or unseen.

To protect and renew your mind you must protect your eye and ear gates because they will be the first points of attack. (Remember Satan in the garden of Eden was able to talk to

Eve, (using her ear gates) and Eve looked at the apple, (with her eyes) and saw that it was good for fruit, (2). If you wish to be successful in renewing your mind you must understand that every experience and everything that you see and hear becomes a small part of you. The company you choose to keep, the relationships you choose to form will either help you grow, develop, and encourage you or keep you depressed, afraid, addicted and bound. Now that you are in the process of renewing your mind, all the old toxic people, places and things must go. You cannot heal successfully around the toxic things and relationships that played a role in your mental anguish. Starting this process (by asking for help) is challenging enough. After this you must start identifying (with the help of a licensed therapist) and uprooting those negative external (and internal) voices from your mind and life. These voices/experiences might be connected to a familiar place, family member, friends or even a career. Prayerfully consider what needs to go by using the spirit of discernment. God is going to be with you during this process beloved, because it is his will that we all prosper and be in good health even as our souls prosper (3).

The word of God and good thoughts are the best fuel and food for your mind. Worship, thanksgiving, and prayer are the best fuel for your soul. If you do not have a personal relationship with Christ, I encourage you to start one today. The prayer at the end of this chapter will help you do that. Beloved you were created to prosper mentally, physically, and spiritually. If you need to reconnect with Christ after being separated from him by willful sin and disobedience it is as simple as asking for forgiveness, having a repentant heart, renouncing all sin in both word and deed, and purposely moving forward in complete faith and obedience to God.

Remember this is not really a mental break down. This is your new beginning! A chance to take a close look at all the things that may have caused you to encounter so much mental and emotional pain and toss them out. I made the mistake of viewing my emotional break down as a sign of weakness and a lack of self-control. I felt embarrassed and humiliated. But as I prayerfully began to do the hard work of healing and rebuilding, I realized that the way I viewed my mental break was wrong and was not going to help me get better. So, I started to view it differently, I began to view it as a chance to look at and get rid of the things that no longer served me. Today, as I look back, I view it as my mind telling me "*Stephanie your life is out of order and the ways you have been living and thinking are causing you terrible emotional, mental and spiritual distress. Stop!*" I was thankful for this because it had become clear to me (and everyone else) that the choices and decisions I was making at the time were the result of being emotionally damaged and in extreme mental anguish.

My mental breakdown was the result of my toxic internal and external landscape. Before my break down I took on battles and carried cares I should have given to God. Because I held on to pain, trauma, and negative experiences, I unknowingly relived them every day for 25 years. I became bitter and angry instead of extending forgiveness and grace to those who hurt and offended me, including myself. I freely gave my help, love, time, and money to people who were only in my life for what they could get (and I knew this). But in my mind, I was convinced that being in these toxic relationships was a lot better than loneliness. I soaked up everyone's negative opinions about me and my life, believing them and letting them define my life and limit my abilities. I would repeatedly replay the negative words of others in my mind trying to figure out whether they were true or not. Adding to all of this was the generational curse I was unknowingly operating under (I was repeating the mistakes of past generations). I thought my mistakes and decisions were normal because other woman in my family had made the same ones before me.

The worst part of all of this was that my relationship with Christ had been severed, mainly because I had been deeply hurt by "church people" and had let this hurt make me angry and bitter. Instead of setting boundaries and extending forgiveness to those who offended me, I vowed never to go back to church again. My thinking was that *I did not need to find the same hurt in church that I found in the world.* The dangerous thing about this thinking was that I had not yet learned how to worship, pray, and live a righteous life outside of the church walls. So, for me living a life without regular church attendance meant falling back into a life of sin separated from God.

Thankfully, God healed me in all these areas, after my mental breakdown, when I completely surrendered them all to him. My mental breakdown forced me to completely surrender all my ashes and brokenness to God and I am better today because of this. Once I broke down completely, I allowed the spirit of God to come in and rebuild me His way. A way in which he would get the glory out of my new life. Since I have done this, my life has been amazing.

I am going to say something radical here; I am going to suggest that if you find yourself facing a mental crisis or breakdown, that you do not feel ashamed or embarrassed but that you embrace it. See it as an opportunity to relinquish control of your life and hand it completely over to God. (After all He knows what is best for your life). Give your broken (down) mental pieces to God so that he can help you rebuild a life that will exceed your expectations. Take this time of mental renewal to renew your relationship with Christ. He is in the business of creating something wonderfully amazing out of darkness and nothingness. Darkness and void were the original conditions of the Earth before God turned it into something amazing by his spirit (4). When your life and mind feel dark and full of nothingness let God breathe on them with his spirit and watch miracles begin to take place. Just as God formed the world in the beginning, once you give your broken pieces to him, he only needs 6 days to recalibrate and renew your mind and create something wonderful out of your life (5). Because God does everything good you will see that letting his spirit renew and strengthen you will help you take control of your mental health and turn you into a peaceful, prosperous, blessed individual.

CHAPTER 2 PRAYER POINT: SINNERS PRAYER

Father God I ask that you forgive me for my sins and the sins of my fathers. Forgive me for turning away from you and living my life in sin and disobedience. I believe in you, and I believe in the power of your death, burial, and resurrection. I believe that my sins have been forgiven and washed away by your precious blood. I accept you as my Lord and Savior. I denounce all sin and disobedience. I fully accept your truth as my truth and your strength as my strength. Help me to live a live that is pleasing and acceptable to you. Renew my mind, heart, and spirit. Remind me every day during this process that I am strong, and that I can do all thing with your help and your strength. In Jesus name I pray and receive these things. Amen

Chapter 3

A New Life

> Therefor if any man be in Christ Jesus, he is a new creature: old things are passed away: behold, all things become new (1)

Repairing, Restoring, Renewing all Things

Developing a new mindset after a mental crisis is not easy, it may take years of intense therapy often paired with medication, patience, prayer, and the Holy Spirit. During this time, you must be gentle and forgiving of yourself and others. Do not get offended easily or frustrated easily. Trust that if God has brought you through the mental darkness that He will continue to carry you into the full light of his righteousness.

The deeper the pain and trauma the longer it will take to experience complete healing, renewal, and restoration. But if you find yourself at the place of mental crisis or mental exhaustion, count it all joy. God is simply asking you to get rid of your old ways of thinking (that are causing you pain, torment, and dis-ease) and put on a new way of thinking, His way. A way of righteousness, peace, and joy in the holy spirit (2). While you are doing the work of restoring your mind, you must also learn how to properly care for your body (the physical realm) and your soul (the spiritual realm).

Nourish (The Body)

In the previous chapters we discussed, in-depth, how to care for the mind. Now we will briefly discuss how to take better care of our bodies and spirits. This is important because the mind, body, and spirit work together. On this new journey to mental wellness, you may also need to renew the ways that you feed your body and spirit. For example, did you know that eating certain foods can help you fight off colds and depression because of the vitamins and minerals these foods contain? Did you know that over-eating is a symptom of anxiety, and that over-eating often leads to obesity? (3) Obesity can lead to a number of serious health problems including heart disease (according to the Center for Disease Control heart disease is the leading cause of death in women) diabetes, stroke, and some types of cancers (4).

This information may seem overwhelming, but it is here as a source of wisdom. Remember during this journey, you are going to take one step at a time. You may only have the strength and resources to eat healthy 2 to 3 days a week. Start when and where you can and remember to do all things with prayer, patience, and thanksgiving. To give you a better understanding about how everything we do plays a role in our ability to maintain our mental health think about it this way: the thoughts we think (which is the food that we feed our minds) and the food we put in our bodies will either fight disease or cause disease in us. If you eat foods that are high in saturated fats or highly processed, you could put your physical health in jeopardy. Poor health and obesity will lead to internal thoughts and feelings of sadness, fear, and depression. Do you see how everything we do can affect our mental and emotional health? It is important to know how to maintain good health mentally, physically, and spiritually to ensure that you experience exceeding joy, prosperity, and complete abundant health. The scripture is worth repeating, *beloved I wish that you prosper and be in good health even as your soul prospers* (5).

Do you know what a proper diet consists of? Do you know what should be on your plate and what should never be on your plate? Let us look at it from a biblical perspective, in the beginning God told Adam and Eve: “See, I have given you plants that give the seeds that are on the Earth, and every tree that has fruit that gives seeds, they will be your food (6). In this scripture we see that the original foods that God provided for us consisted of only fruit and herbs (vegetables). Fruit and herbs should be incorporated into every meal you eat. According to one study done by The Harvard School of Public Health, (2021) a diet rich in vegetables and fruit can lower blood pressure, reduce the risk of heart disease and stroke, prevent some types of cancer, lower the risk of eye and digestive problems, and have a positive effect upon blood sugar, which can help keep your appetite in check. Eating non-starchy vegetables and fruits like apples, pears, and green leafy vegetables may even promote weight loss because their low glycemic loads prevent blood sugar spikes that can increase hunger (7). As you begin to move forward and renew your life, start replacing foods high in salt and sugar with fruits and vegetable. This will enhance your physical health which is a part of your overall health.

In the beginning of my journey to better mental health, God through the holy spirit spoke to me about letting go of certain foods. For almost 15 years I was plagued by violent nightmares and sleep paralysis. I could never understand why and always thought it was rooted in the demonic. One night, (after God had begun the process of helping me restore and renew my mind) I made a meal that consisted of ground beef (which comes out of the package red, raw and bloody). I cooked the meat and enjoyed the meal with my children. That night I had the most violent, bloody nightmare I had ever had. I woke up and thought *God why?* Please show me why I am dreaming these things and how to stop dreaming them? I immediately heard the holy spirit direct me to stop eating red meat and pork and my nightmares would stop. I gave it a shot and decided to stop eating those meats for 2 weeks (opting for ground turkey instead). I did not have one nightmare or bad dream during those two weeks. I was amazed, and instantly healed from 15 years of nightmares. Up until then I thought nightmares were just a part of my life and that I would have to get used to them. No! This is not the way God intended for us to sleep. He did not intend for us to be plagued by nightmares and night terrors during our rest. In fact, the bible says "when you lay down, thou shall not be afraid: Yea, thou shall lie down, and thy sleep shall be sweet (8). Sleep paralysis and night terrors were my experience for many years. You may have been or continue to be plagued by something different. Whatever it is, I assure you my friend, God is ready and able to deliver you from all that troubles you if you simply ask, wait patiently for the answer, and have faith that he will deliver you.

(Nourish) The Soul

"Do you not know that your body is the temple of the Holy Spirit within you, whom ye have from God? Ye are not your own, but you are bought with a price" (9). Just like our mind, our physical body needs daily maintenance. Our physical bodies need proper exercise, rest, diet, and sunlight. I will not talk much more about maintaining good physical health, but I will say that good physical health is necessary to perform our reasonable service to this world and the Lord (10). If we are over-weight, diabetic, plagued with high blood pressure and other preventable diseases we cannot be as effective or as active in our daily lives.

Although our souls are housed within our bodies, our soul and spirit require very different nutrients and maintenance than those required by the mind and body to grow, mature, and develop. Salvation is protection for the soul in this world (11). Water baptism is an important part of a believer's life according to scripture (12). Prayer, or communication with God, is the main sustainer of the soul and must be constant (13). The indwelling of the Holy Spirit shields, protects, and comforts the human soul while it is in this world until the day it is redeemed in the second coming of Jesus Christ. I do not want to get too deep into this subject. I simply want to give you a clear understanding of how the mind, body and soul are connected and how to keep each of them healthy and disease free.

While we are working on renewing our minds we must try, as much as possible to also renew, nourish and properly care for our bodies and souls. Renewing your mind and recovering from a mental crisis is a life-long journey. It is a process with no real end date. Every day we gain more insight and a better understanding, we gain more wisdom, and we grow in faith and grace. Every day we seek to grow into spiritually mature adults, who can be used by God to bless, love, and edify other people. The more we let get of our pride, ego's, fleshly desires, and expectations, the more we will see the will of God and the blessings of God in our lives. Lastly, if you are dealing with stubborn sin that seems to reappear in your life or the lives of your children it may be something that requires prayer coupled with fasting. The Bible declares that some things (sin and generational curses) can only come out by prayer that is coupled with fasting (14). Please consult your physician if you have any underlying health conditions that may get worse if you choose to fast. Remember that fasting can be done 2 to 3 hours at a time. It can consist of water only or a liquid fast (soups and broths). Fasting has physical health benefits as well and you will find that your spiritual strength will increase during a fast. Beloved, you are responsible for maintaining your mental, emotional, spiritual, and physical health. When you take care of yourself you can be a blessing and an asset to yourself, your family, your community, and the Kingdom of God.

CHAPTER 3 PRAYER POINT:

Father I thank you for making all things new. I thank you for this life you have given me, for this mind you have given me and this spirit you have given me. With your help I seek to renew my mind, body, and spirit. I ask you to create in me a clean heart and renew a right spirit and mind within me. A spirit that seeks to worship you and a mind that thirsts after your truth. I ask these things in Jesus' name I pray this prayer. Amen.

Chapter 4

The Dawning of a New Day

> But the God of all grace who has called us into his eternal glory by Christ Jesus, after ye have suffered a while, make you perfect, establish, strengthen, and settle you (1).

Imagine (for a moment) the darkest hours for the first followers of Jesus. They walked with him for many years, were taught by him, feed by him, watched him restore sight to the blind and life to the dead. Here it is day 2 after his crucifixion. All hope seemed lost. Not only had Jesus been murdered for preaching the truth, but his murderers also began hunting down the disciples who closely followed him.

The darkest hour comes for us all. That time of unexplainable suffering, when nothing makes sense in our lives and God has seemed to go quiet. A time when we start to question all that we have ever believed simply because of this darkness. What do we do in the dark times of a mental crisis? Be still, pray and continue to trust in and believe God for better days to come. This is something I had to do. However, my time of stillness, prayer, and belief lasted 15 years. During those 15 years, it seemed like God was never going to answer me or deliver me out of my mental anguish and addictions.

Have you been asking for and seeking a mental resurrection? Have you been praying for the restoration of a parodical child, or your finances? Are you lacking hope, strength, faith, and courage? Be of good courage, there is hope! But often before the dawning of that hope you will experience the darkest hour. Your faith is important during dark times. Faith allows us to see what we hope for when our natural eyes are beholding only chaos and turmoil. It allows us to look beyond the present sufferings and hope for a brighter future. Faith says: if you can believe that things will be better (even though they look bad now) then they will be better. Always pray for things to turn around and when you pray do not doubt, no matter how long you have been praying for the turn around. Turn your pain into a reason to go boldly to the throne of grace where there is mercy waiting for you.

Never lose hope because God specializes in resurrecting dead things. He likes to flex his miracle muscles by doing exceedingly and abundantly above all we could ever ask or imagine. If you keep the faith and speak openly and honestly to God letting Him know that you still believe Him for mental restoration, financial healing, physical healing, and you start doing the work required to achieve those things, I guarantee you friend that He will answer you and exceed your wildest expectations. I am a witness to this, as it has happened in my own life.

Faith & Vision

Faith was created for the times when you cannot see how *it* is going to happen, or how you will ever be healed, Faith is the vision that will allow you to say *"Yes, Lord, I actually do see it and believe it."* Do not ever lose your hope and faith, especially if you are facing a metal crisis. Do not lose faith because you think the healing process is taking too long. Faith is the only currency that is accepted in the spirit realm. You can exchange it for anything you need help you grow in grace and in the knowledge of our Lord and Savior (2).

The Bible defines faith as *the substance of things we hope for and evidence of the things we cannot yet see* (4). As you begin, with the help of the holy spirit, to unpack and get rid of the mental baggage of past hurts, trauma, and disappointments there is one bag that I want you to pick up and fill daily, your bag of faith. In this bag I want you to place all your hopes, dreams, and visions for your future. I talk a lot about faith in this section because it is the only vehicle that will get you from the place of renewing your mind to walking and living in that newness of mind.

Remember that faith without works is dead (5), meaning that, you can have faith that God will give you financial freedom, but you must do the saving, tithing, and cleaning up of your credit. It means that you can have faith that God will help you renew your mind, but you must stop filling it with garbage and allowing other people to fill it with their garbage. Another part of the mind renewal process is the ability to look at your future in a new light (through the lens of faith and hope). When you view yourself and your new life through the lens of faith, you no longer see yourself or your future through the lens of other peoples' negative opinions of you or through the lens of the negative things that have happened to you. For example, a rape victim may feel dirty and unlovable, so they carry themselves and view themselves as a dirty, unlovable individual because they are viewing themselves through the traumatic experience. While renewing your mind you will need to change this thinking and narrative in your mind. What happened to you (or what people have said about you) has nothing to do with your identity as a person. It is not your identity; it is a negative experience or a negative opinion. Remember the first mental attack on Adam and Eve by Satan, he made them believe that there was something so wrong with who they were and how they were made that they felt ashamed enough to hide from their creator. The enemy is still up to his old tricks. He is out to distort our self-image by creating situations that will make us feel dirty, worthless, and ashamed. Be aware of Satan's tricks by praying always and using the spirit of discernment to weed through the enemy's lies and avoid negative situations in the future. The grace and mercy of God says you are redeemed, loved, important, and more than a conqueror. I no longer view myself as dirty because of rape (although it took me 20 years to stop viewing myself this way). I now understand that a bad thing happened to me, but I do not have to let it continue to define me or hold me captive. I have forgiven my abuser and I have asked God for the grace to live my life in the light and knowledge of his grace and love.

We can untangle ourselves from the hurts of our past with the help of the Holy Spirit and we can learn to think clearly, speak honestly, and love ourselves and others genuinely. But we must do these things through the strength of Christ. He is our healer, and it his will that we prosper and be healthy in every way. Spiritual healing begins by renewing our mind, and the effects of this healing will flow into the natural (or physical) realm. Be encouraged as you begin to renew your mind and take control of your thoughts. With the help of the Holy spirit along with some patience and self-love you can start to develop a healthy sound mind.

A New Day Begins with a New Mindset

Dawn is the most beautiful time of day. It is a time of prayer, stillness, and reflection. It brings a new hope that the new day that lies ahead will be filled with blessings and answered prayers. Once you begin to see the dawning of a new day in your mental health, you will notice that the old toxic thoughts, people, places, and conversations you once tolerated now irritate your spirit and you no longer desire to be a part of them. You will prefer solitude instead of negative company. You will desire the things of God more than the things of this world. You will not be easily offended. You will desire and seek after growth, peace, understanding, patience, righteousness, forgiveness, love, hope, and humility.

The spirit of humility is a very important spiritual attribute to possess while you are in the process of renewing your mind. Humility is a form of self-control, and self-control is a fruit of the spirit (3). Humility does not need to be the center of attention. It does not need to be right or have the last word. Having the spirit of humility will help you let many negative things go and choose peace over being right or being recognized. Having a humble spirit will get you favor and grace faster than having a mind filled with pride and arrogance. Take care of yourself by taking care of your thoughts.

CHAPTER 4 PRAYER POINT:

The Lord bless you and keep you: The Lord make His face to shine upon you and be gracious unto you: The Lord lift up His countenance upon you and give you peace. (6).

Part 3

Review

In life there may come a time, due to trauma after trauma and disappointment after disappointment, that we will find ourselves in a mental crisis, or suffering from a mental disease. A dark time in life where it seems we are having one wilderness experience after another. Where midnight seems to last for years, and no one is around to understand or lend a hand. We have prayed and prayed but it seems like God is just not listening. We become bitter, angry, resentful, and depressed. We begin to carry these emotions around allowing them to seep into our conversations, relationships and even distort our self-perceptions and extinguish our hopes for a bright future. (Note: having a tough time or facing a challenge does not always lead to a mental crisis. Depending on the severity of the crisis or trauma, length of time, and our mental capability, we might be able to overcome many challenges and small afflictions.) But when we are already weak spiritually, emotionally, and mentally the attacks of the enemy can cause catastrophic damage to our mental health.

It is during these dark times that we will find the light of God if we get still, and allow His understanding, love, light. and presence into our lives. There is no one way out of mental and spiritual darkness (or crisis) expect to go through it. It will feel like the valley of the shadow of death, but remember, God is right there with you (1). You must believe that you are not going through it alone.

There is something that God has given us to help during dark times; It is called Faith. Faith is filled with the things we hope for, and the things that we cannot yet see. That is why it is most useful when all we are seeing with our natural eyes is darkness and sadness. Faith is activated when we cannot see how we will ever get out of poverty or mental anguish. Your faith says: I cannot see how this is going to happen, but my faith says it will. Faith asks us to activate our imagination.

For a moment I want you to visualize what you want your future to look like. Do not base your vision on what is currently going on in your life but use your faith. For example, you may currently have a negative balance in your bank account, and because of this negative balance you may believe and visualize a future that is filled with nothing but poverty and hopelessness. Faith asks you to believe the exact opposite. Use your faith to believe that no matter how things look now you will enjoy a future of financial freedom where you will be able to lend to the poor and needy and still have enough to live comfortably. Situations that seem impossible and look dark are the very things that activate our faith.

While renewing your mind, prayer will be your companion and faith will be the vehicle that will always lead you out of dark situations. Be patient with yourself. Do not put a time limit on your mental healing. Trust God and trust his timing. The main goal here is to gain control of your thoughts and emotions instead of letting them control you, hold you hostage, and dictate your behavior. Jesus died so that we can be free from emotional bondage and experience superior mental, physical and spiritual health.

We must examine ourselves, our thinking, our motives, and our intentions every day and make sure we are operating from a place of love and compassion. Remember that loving yourself must happen before you can love your neighbor. Viewing yourself in a loving way takes place in the mind. So often life will throw things our way that make us doubt who we are and how much we are worth. Beloved, you are valuable and are worth more than rubies. Remember that when things happen that make you doubt your worth these things are sent from Satan to kill your joy, steal your confidence, and destroy your peace. Rebuke these thoughts and do not give them a place in your mind or heart. You are fearfully and wonderfully made (2). When you are feeling discouraged at any point during this mental and emotional healing process pray for strength and read through the book of Psalms. God is with you as he promised he would be (3).

It is my prayer that you learn how important your mental health is and that you learn how to control and maintain your thoughts and emotions. I join my faith with yours in believing for good health and prosperity. The following reflection section has been provided for you to write down your thoughts, visions, dreams and hopes for the future. I encourage you to write and be open and honest with God and yourself. This life is your journey. Partner with God to make it a great one.

Part 3

Notes & Reflection

Date: ____________________

In all these things we are more than conquerors through him that loved us (5).

Endnotes

Introduction

1. Proverbs 4:23 KJV.
2. Romans 12:2 KJV.
3. Mark 6:37-39 KJV.
4. John 10:10 NKJV.
5. Isaiah 61:1-3 KJV.
6. 2 Corinthians 12:8 KJV.

Part 1 Chapter 1

1. 2 Corinthians 10:5 KJV.
2. "The Mind." Oxford Languages Dictionary. 2021. http://Languages.oup.com/google/dictionary-en/
3. Isaiah 26:3, KJV.
4. Genesis 3 KJV.
5. Genesis 3:5-6 KJV.
6. Genesis 3:4 KJV.
7. Genesis 3:7 KJV.
8. Genesis 2:25 KJV.
9. Genesis 3:7 KJV.
10. Genesis 1:17 & Psalms 139:14 KJV.
11. Hebrews 4:16 KJV.

12. Psalms 139:14 KJV.
13. Ephesians 6:17 KJV.
14. Genesis 2:17 KJV.
15. Genesis 3:23 KJV.
16. 2 Corinthians 5:7 NIV.
17. Ephesians 4:26 KJV.
18. Proverbs 4:7 KJV.

Part 1 Chapter 2

1. Psalms 1:1-2 KJV.
2. Genesis 1:27 KJV.
3. Romans 8:6 KJV.
4. Psalms 1:1-2 KJV.
5. "Meditate." Oxford Languages Dictionary. 2021. http://Languages.oup.com/google/dictionary-en/
6. Psalms 1:2 KJV.

Part 1 Chapter 3

1. Philippians 4:8 KJV.
2. Zechariah 4:6 KJV.
3. Luke 23:34 KJV.
4. Hebrews 12:14-16 NIV.
5. Exodus 2:3 KJV.
6. John 14:12 NIV.
7. Philippians 4:8 KJV.
8. Galatians 5:22 KJV.
9. Philippians 2:5 KJV.

Part 1 Chapter 4

1. Luke 13:19 KJV.
2. Matthew 13:23 KJV.
3. "Till." Oxford Languages Dictionary. 2021. http://languages.oup.com/google/dictionary-en/
4. 1 Thessalonians 5:16-18 KJV.
5. Matthew 7:17 KJV.
6. 1 Thessalonians 5:18 NIV.
7. "Discernment." Oxford Languages Dictionary. 2021. http://languages.oup.com/google/dictionary-en/
8. Philippians 4:13 KJV.
9. Joshua 1:8 NIV.
10. 1 Peter 5:7 NIV.

Review

1. 3 John 2 NKJV.
2. James 1:22 NIV.
3. Proverbs 3:13 NIV.
4. Isaiah 6:13 KJV.
5. Proverbs 4:7 KJV.

Part 2 Chapter 1

1. Hebrews 12:1-2 KJV.
2. Matthew 13:3-8 KJV.
3. Philippians 1:6 KJV.
4. 1 Corinthians 11:28 & Matthew 7:5 KJV.
5. James 1:8 NIV.

Part 2 Chapter 2

1. Luke 10:38-42 KJV.
2. Luke 6:45 NIV.

Part 2 Chapter 3

1. 1 John 4:1 KJV.
2. "Boundary." Oxford Languages Dictionary. 2021. http://languauges.oup.com/google/dictionary-en/
3. Romans 8:11 KJV.
4. Hebrews 11:7-11 KJV.
5. Acts 2:46 KJV.
6. James 2:17 KJV.
7. 1 Corinthians 10:4 NIV.

Part 2 Chapter 4

1. Psalms 23:2-3 KJV.
2. Matthew 8:23-27 KJV.
3. Luke 6:45 KJV.
4. Exodus 20:8-11 KJV.

Review

1. "Dis." Oxford Languages Dictionary. 2021. http://languages.oup.com/google/dictionary-en/
2. Hebrews 12:1 NIV.

Part 3 Chapter 1

1. 2 Corinthians 12:8 KJV.

2. Navigating a Mental Health Crisis, 2018. Retrieved from: https://www.nami.org/About-Mental-Illness/Warning-Signs-and-Symptoms
3. Philippians 4:13 KJV.
4. Philippians 1:6 KJV.
5. 1 Peter 5:7 NIV.

Part 3 Chapter 2

1. Philippians 2:5 KJV.
2. Genesis 3:6KJV.
3. 3 John 1:2 KJV.
4. Genesis 1:2-31 NIV.
5. Exodus 20:11 KJV.

Part 3 Chapter 3

1. 2 Corinthians 5:17 KJV.
2. Romans 14:17 NKJV.
3. Eating Recovery Center, 2021. Retrieved from: https://www.eatingrecoverycenter.com/resources/patients
4. CDC, 2021. Retrieved from: https://www.cdc.gov/heartdisease/about/htm
5. 3 John 2:4 KJV.
6. Genesis 1:29 KJV.
7. Harvard School of Public Health, 2021. The Nutrition Source. Retrieved from: https://www.hsph.harvard.edu/nutritionsource/what-should-you-eat/vegetables-and-fruits/
8. Proverbs 3:24 KJV.

9. 1 Corinthians 1:29 KJV.
10. Romans 12:1 KJV.
11. Romans 10:9-10 KJV.
12. Matthew 28:29 NIV.
13. Luke 18:1 KJV.
14. Matthew 17:21 KJV.

Part 3 Chapter 4

1. 1 Peter 5:10 KJV.
2. 2 Peter 3:18 KJV.
3. Galatians 5:22 KJV.
4. Hebrews 11:1 KJV.
5. James 2:17 KJV.
6. Numbers 6:26 KJV.

Review

1. Psalms 23:4 KJV.
2. Psalms 139:14 KJV.
3. Matthew 28:20 KJV.
4. Psalms 139:4 NIV.
5. Romans 8:38 KJV.

Mental Health Resources

- The National Alliance for Mental Health
  www.nami.org or 1-800-950-NAMI (6264)
- National Suicide Prevention Helpline
  1-800-273-8255
- For on-line help with mental health issues
  please visit: http://www.rethink.org
- Addiction and Recovery Helpline
  1-800-662-4357

Scriptures for Daily Challenges

Afraid/Fear	Hebrews 11:1
Anxiousness	Philippians 4:6-7
Bitterness	Ephesians 4:31
Depressed	Isaiah 41:10
Discouraged	Joshua 1:9
Doubt/Worry	Matthew 6:28-29
Disappointment	Joshua 10:25
Sadness	Revelation 21:4
Forgiveness	Ephesians 4:31-32
Guilt	Isaiah 54:4
Failure	Joshua 1:9
Finances	Proverbs 13:11
Rejection	John 1:11
Sin	1 John 1:8-10
Hurt/Pain	1 Peter 5:10
Sickness	Jeremiah 17:14
Death	1 Corinthians 15:51-52
Prayer	Luke 18:1, Ephesians 6:18

About the Author

Stephanie Jackson has dedicated her life to helping those who are suffering emotionally, spiritually, and mentally. She earned her master's degree in criminal justice in 2019. Renewing your Mind is the first of many inspirational, uplifting and encouraging books.

www.ingramcontent.com/pod-product-compliance
Lightning Source LLC
Chambersburg PA
CBHW030155070426
42447CB00031B/466
* 9 7 8 0 5 7 8 9 0 4 0 1 6 *